SAP R/3 and
Oracle Backup and Recovery

SAP R/3 and Oracle Backup and Recovery

Greg Spence

 Addison-Wesley

An imprint of PEARSON EDUCATION

Harlow, England · Reading, Massachusetts · Menlo Park, California · New York · Don Mills, Ontario · Amsterdam · Bonn
Sydney · Singapore · Tokyo · Madrid · San Juan · Milan · Mexico City · Seoul · Taipei

PEARSON EDUCATION LIMITED

Head Office:
Edinburgh Gate
Harlow CM20 2JE
Tel: +44 (0)1279 623623
Fax: +44 (0)1279 431059

London Office:
128 Long Acre, London WC2E 9AN
Tel: +44 (0)171 447 2000
Fax: +44 (0)171 240 5771

First published in Great Britain 1999

© Pearson Education Limited 1999

The rights of Greg Spence to be identified as author of this work have been asserted by him in accordance with the Copyright, Designs, and Patents Act 1988.

ISBN 0-201-59622-9

British Library Cataloguing in Publication Data
A CIP catalogue record for this book can be obtained from the British Library.

Library of Congress Cataloging in Publication Data
Applied for.

The programs in this book have been included for their instructional value. They have been tested with care but are not guaranteed for any particular purpose. The publisher does not offer any warranties or representations nor does it accept any liabilities with respect to the programs.

Many of the designations used by manufacturers and sellers to distinguish their products are claimed as trademarks. Pearson Education Limited has made every attempt to supply trademark information about manufacturers and their products mentioned in this book. A list of the trademark designations and their owners appears on this page.

Trademark notice
Oracle is a trademark of Oracle Corporation. Informise and Informise Online are trademarks of Informise Corporation. Microsoft SQL Server is a trademark of Microsoft Corporation. DB2, AIX, OS/390 are trademarks of International Business Machines Corporation. Adabas D is a trademark of Adabas AG. All other products are trademarks of their respective holders.
SAP, R/3, ABAP/4, SAP Archivelink and SAP Business Workflow are registered trademarks of SAP Aktiengesellschaft Systems, Applications and Products in Data Processing, Neurottstraße 16, D-69190 Walldorf, Germany. The publisher gratefully acknowledges SAP's kind permission to use its trademark in this publication. SAP AG is not the publisher of this book and is not responsible for it under any aspect of press law.

10 9 8 7 6 5 4 3 2 1

Typeset by Pantek Arts, Maidstone, Kent.
Printed and bound in Great Britain by Biddles Ltd., Guildford & Kings Lynn.

The Publishers' policy is to use paper manufactured from sustainable forests.

Contents

7 Disaster recovery considerations   **151**

8 Backup and recovery examples   **159**

9 Future trends and directions   **172**

Bibliography   **174**

Acknowledgments

No book can be produced in isolation, and that is certainly true of this one. I would like to thank, first and foremost, my wife Katrina, my daughter Katherine, and my son Alex for the support they have given me over the many months it took me to produce the first draft.

I would like to thank my employers, PLATINUM technology, inc. headquarters in Oakbrook Terrace, Chicago, Illinois, USA, for providing the environment within which the production of this book was possible. I would also like to thank SAP for providing me with the high quality source material available on their comprehensive SAPnet website at *http://sapnet.sap_ag.de* which keeps me updated with the latest and greatest information on R/3.

Last but not least, I would like to thank my publisher, Addison-Wesley Longman, and in particular Steve Temblett, Commissioning Editor, for his faith in me and in the draft chapters which started all of this! I would like to thank Bridget Allen, Managing Editor, and the production department in Harlow for all their hard work in getting the book into print and the numerous people who reviewed the manuscript and its various revisions.

As usual, any errors or omissions are entirely on my part.

Greg Spence
Southampton, Hants

Introduction

SAP is currently the world leader in ERP (Enterprise Resource Planning) software solutions, with the majority of the Fortune 500 companies using SAP R/3 as one of their core applications. The powerful range of functions supplied by R/3 is one of the main reasons for its success, the other is the adoption by SAP of industry standard interfaces.

This book concentrates on perhaps the most important area of SAP R/3 administration, Backup and Recovery.

How this book is structured

This book is divided into several chapters covering the following topics:

Chapter 1 – discusses the background to why SAP R/3 backup and recovery is important, gives some reasons as to why failures occur, and discusses some basic backup approaches a DBA can take.

Chapter 2 – covers the SAP R/3 architecture in detail.

Chapter 3 – covers the Oracle architecture as implemented with SAP R/3.

Chapter 4 – discusses configuring SAP R/3 and Oracle. It covers guidelines for the installation of R/3, explains the Oracle Parallel Server architecture and discusses some issues surrounding Oracle VLDBs (Very Large Databases).

Chapter 5 – covers SAP R/3 backup in detail.

Chapter 6 – covers SAP R/3 recovery in detail.

Chapter 7 – discusses disaster recovery planning and implementation, including the Oracle Hot Standby architecture, the SAP Zero Downtime Project and critical R/3 maintenance steps.

Chapter 8 – provides some real-life examples of database failures and how they are resolved.

Chapter 9 – looks at future trends and directions for SAP R/3 backup and recovery.

1 Backup and recovery concepts

1.1 The need to backup regularly

It is a fact today that Oracle databases are getting larger! As corporations throughout the world implement their core applications on top of the Oracle RDBMS, implement ever increasing numbers of Data Warehouses, and keep more of their data online, the problems of managing those databases increase proportionately.

The DBA faces many new challenges. Corporations now require their applications, and hence their database management systems, to be available 24 hours per day, 7 days per week, 365 days per year. They expect performance to be maintained, irrespective of the increasing data volumes, and the system to undergo routine maintenance without any downtime. A very tall order!

Add to this the complexity of an Enterprise Resource Planning (ERP) application such as SAP R/3 and the need for a planned and effective backup and recovery mechanism becomes much more important.

1.1.1 How databases fail

Any DBA who has had to restore a crashed database will know the problems he/she has to face if suitable backup and recovery procedures are not put in place. According to Oracle worldwide support, out of all severity 1 database down problems:

- 36% of them are caused by software bugs;

- 34% are caused by poor DBA skills, user errors, improper database setup and inadequate backup procedures;

- 30% result from physical failure such as disk crashes and CPU failures.

The figures also reveal that when a failure occurs, the average length of time it takes a DBA to return the database to an operational state is 18 hours! This is due to the fact that either the DBA does not know how to recover from a problem (and therefore makes the matter worse by trying to recover incorrectly), or does not have an adequate backup to recover all transactions without loss of data.

If this situation existed 20 years ago it may not have been considered critical due to the fact that a lengthy period of downtime was almost expected in the days of mainly batch-oriented environments. In today's online, real-time world, and bearing in mind the average corporation's dependence on its computer technology, this situation is far from acceptable yet the above figures come from recent information supplied by some of the largest Oracle customer sites in the world.

Planning, designing and implementing a secure and robust backup and recovery mechanism for both Oracle and SAP R/3 is essential, but not easy. Very few DBAs are able to successfully implement all or part of such a mechanism.

Why should this be?

It is partly down to inexperience, lack of time, and a failure to adequately test the recovery mechanism to see if it works effectively or works at all before disaster strikes! Furthermore, implementing hot standby databases, testing recovery procedures and maintaining adequate backup practices takes detailed knowledge of both R/3 and Oracle, not to mention a great deal of effort.

This is where this book can help by explaining everything a DBA needs to ensure a smooth running database system with close to zero downtime.

1.1.2 Taking out an insurance policy

Given the growing importance of the SAP R/3 system within an organization, it is important to consider protecting the hardware and software from failure by building in hardware and software redundancy.

Hardware redundancy is provided by utilizing a second machine on another site and taking advantage of the Hot Standby Database available from Release 7.3. Other measures that can be taken include:

- using disk arrays;

- using an Uninterruptable Power Supply (UPS).

Software redundancy is provided by mirroring control files, redo logs, and keeping on- and offline backup copies of the archive logs. There is no substitute for a thorough backup and recovery policy reviewed on a regular basis. Database disasters should be simulated on a test machine, using a database architecture that is identical to the production system, and practicing different types of recovery. We will illustrate different problems that can occur with your database system and demonstrate different recovery methods that can be used to recover from such problems later.

1.1.3 Backup approaches

Backups can be divided into two types, physical and logical. Physical backups involve taking actual copies of the operating system files, or UNIX raw devices, and placing them on a backup device, such as tape. A physical backup can be further categorized into an online and offline backup, more commonly known as a hot and cold backup respectively. A hot backup is performed whilst the database is open and being used, cold backups are performed after the database has been shut down.

Logical backups take copies of the database objects and data using SQL commands. The data can be imported back into the same database or into another database if required. DBAs normally perform logical backups using the Oracle Export/Import utility.

1.1.4 Oracle's new backup/recovery tool

Shipped with Oracle8 is a new product called Recovery Manager. This product can take physical (not logical) backups of your database and obtains the information about what to backup from either the database control file or the recovery catalog, which is a set of database tables. This product is provided to make backup and recovery easier for the DBA and can be controlled either from a command line or from within Oracle's Enterprise Manager DBA tool, which provides a GUI interface.

Recovery Manager uses an API (application programming interface) to operate with third party tape management systems for copying and recovering essential files to and from offline media. We will discuss Recovery Manager in more detail later and use the product to illustrate some of our backup/recovery examples.

1.1.5 Automatic backups

Once you have a well-designed backup strategy in place that works, you can turn your attention to automating it. It is amazing the number of DBAs who still rely on memory, or at best, manually maintained lists when performing backups. A large cause of backup/recovery problems is human error. Why not use the technology we have to reduce or even eliminate human error wherever possible and make our lives as easy as possible? We will address the issue of automation later in this book with some practical examples; here I would like to point out some things to consider when automating your backups.

The majority of DBAs use operating system scripts together with a job submission program such as 'cron' or 'at' in the UNIX world, or third-party job schedulers. If you are using, or planning to use, scripts for your backup automation you should bear the following in mind:

- Make your scripts as generic as possible to reduce the amount of maintenance effort you will need to undergo when upgrading your Oracle software. This can be achieved by using SQL queries within your scripts to obtain object names for backup etc.

- Always, always, always write the progress of your backup to a log file. It is particularly important to timestamp every event so that should a backup script fail you can track where it was in the backup process and the timestamp can be used to determine the exact time of failure.

- Whenever the structure of your database changes, such as adding a new data file to a tablespace, you must remember to modify your backup scripts. If you make them generic using an SQL query to produce the list of data files to backup you will not need to do this.

It is preferable to use a third party backup/recovery tool for the automation of your backup strategy. This way all of the issues raised above will be handled by the product, reducing your maintenance tasks to virtually zero.

This book is intended to increase the level of experience of the DBA – by guiding you step-by-step through the processes required to plan, design and implement a backup and recovery policy for both the SAP R/3 application environment (versions 3.1x and 4.x) and the Oracle RDBMS (releases 7 and 8). After reading this book, you should be in a better position to maintain your mission critical R/3 environment. Throughout this book we will touch on the above topics and where necessary provide solutions to the problems discussed.

2 R/3 architecture

Before we can discuss backup and recovery in detail we need a good understanding of the SAP R/3 architecture. It is important to understand what components make up the R/3 system and how they work together. We shall also take our first look at the backup and recovery tools available for R/3.

2.1 Basic architecture

SAP R/3 is designed to optimally operate in a three-tier client/server architecture although it is more commonly installed on a two-tier architecture.

In a three-tier environment each tier is responsible for one of the following layers:

- presentation
- application
- data storage.

The presentation layer consists of the **SAPGUI** process, which is responsible for handling data input and output and managing the presentation of the data to the user.

The application layer consists of what SAP calls the **Application Server**. This server is responsible for running the following components:

- Dynpro interpreter
- ABAP/4 dialog processes
- dispatcher
- work processes.

The third tier, data storage, is known as the **Database Server**. This is where the database engine executes and can be either Oracle, Informix Online, Microsoft SQL Server, DB2 for AIX, DB2/400, DB2/OS390 or ADABAS D. This book concentrates on the Oracle-based R/3 implementation.

Figure 2.1 illustrates the three-tier architecture.

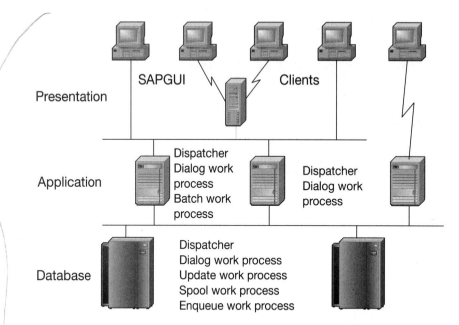

Figure 2.1   Three-tier client server architecture

In a two-tier architecture it is usual for the application and database server to reside on the same machine.

ABAP/4?

2.1.1   The application layer

The application layer is the heart of the R/3 application. It is here where the various processes execute to service users and provide access to the R/3 database server (see Figure 2.2). It is also in this layer where the ABAP/4 programs execute. ABAP/4 is the programming language provided by SAP for the purpose of implementing and modifying the business logic.

Let's take a closer look at each of the processes that go to make up the application server.

Dialog work process

This process is the interface between the user and the R/3 system. It handles requests initiated from the SAPGUI and is responsible for ensuring data returned from such requests is sent back to the user. The process is actually divided into three sub-processes. The **Task Handler** coordinates the activities of the dialog work process and activates either the ABAP/4 or the Dynpro sub-process as needed. The task handler also forms part of the other work processes found on the application server (see Figure 2.2).

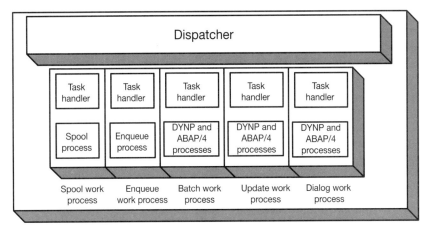

Figure 2.2   R/3 application server

The **Dynpro Interpreter (DYNP)** is responsible for handling the dialog step control. A dialog step is the processing of a single request. For example, a dialog step would consist of a request initiated by a user from one of the SAPGUI screens and end with the return of the data together with the screen layout that is required to display it. The execution of the ABAP/4 code is performed by the **ABAP** sub-process whilst the Dynpro interpreter determines which SAPGUI screen should be used to display the results of the execution.

During dialog step processing the systems will need to access the database. This is achieved via the database interface, which is a constituent part of each work process.

There can be more than one dialog work process per application server.

Batch work process

Background processing forms a large part of the R/3 system. The batch work process is responsible for executing ABAP/4 reports and programs according to a pre-defined schedule or in reaction to some event. The R/3 batch scheduler is responsible for starting the execution of each batch process. In fact the batch scheduler is simply a program executed by a dialog work process. When batch and online dialog work processes are both executing, the online dialog processes are given a higher priority. The batch work process will potentially make heavy use of the database in order to perform its job and the DBA must be aware of the batch schedules in place when planning an appropriate backup strategy.

There can be more than one batch work process.

Spool work process

This process will also access the RDBMS. It is responsible for spooling output to some external device such as a printer or fax machine. It performs its role by copying data out of the database and copying it to a temporary sequential file. It will then invoke the relevant program passing the temporary filename as a parameter.

There is only one spool work process per application server.

Enqueue work process

The enqueue work process is responsible for managing the internal locking of database objects. This locking mechanism is in addition to the locking capabilities provided by the Oracle RDBMS. Oracle, like all relational database systems, locks at a database object level. The requirements of an R/3 system are that locking should be performed at a business level, which will involve multiple database objects and multiple application programs. It is this level that the enqueue work process is responsible for.

In order to avoid performance bottlenecks, the locking is performed and recorded in a lock table stored in main memory. It is not possible therefore for a DBA to be able to see all of the locks being used by simply querying the Oracle performance views (known as the V$ views).

This locking mechanism enables the following functionality:

- Multiple database objects can be locked and treated as a single entity.

- Locks can be held for multiple programs (for example more than one dialog process may be involved in a single transaction for the same user. The enqueue work process would maintain these locks during each change of process).

- In a client/server configuration where there are multiple application servers, each server must be aware of the locks currently in place.

- All locks must be valid system-wide.

- Allows R/3 to be run on multiple processor systems.

In normal cases, only one enqueue work process will perform all of the locking tasks required. However, in order to avoid unnecessary communication between other work processes and the enqueue process, it is possible for the other work processes to perform enqueue and dequeue functions on their own if they are running on the same machine as the enqueue process.

Update work process

Each transaction between a user and a dialog work process can cause many small actions to be performed against the RDBMS. In large R/3 systems, where thousands of users are simultaneously executing transactions, this can cause a massive number of database accesses. In order to minimize the performance impact on the database, the desired updates are written to a log record held in a table in the RDBMS called VBLOG. The update work process is then responsible for reading these log records and applying the changes to the relevant database tables.

In order to understand some of the implications of the R/3 update processes on the RDBMS, and to fully understand how to recover when something goes wrong, it is necessary to understand how updates are applied to the RDBMS.

When a dialog work process needs to update the database, the R/3 dispatcher process (discussed next) writes an update record into the VBLOG table. The dispatcher then initiates an update work process to execute the update against the database. Updates are an asynchronous process, which means they are processed in the order they are received. If for any reason an update cannot complete, the user will get a system message and an express mail. One of the many reasons an update may not complete successfully is due to a full tablespace or the database suddenly failing.

An update log record can have two components, primary and secondary, which are processed according to their importance. Primary updates, known as V1 (the letter 'V' is used because the German word for 'update' begins with this letter), are time-critical and must be completed before the secondary updates (V2). If any V1 update is not processed, its associated V2 components will not be processed either.

If the update fails whilst processing a V1 component, all the work carried out as part of the same R/3 transaction (or Logical Unit of Work – see later for a discussion of this) will be rolled back and a status condition written to the VBLOG table. If the failure occurs processing a V2 component, only the changes associated with that component, will be rolled back and the appropriate V2 record marked with a failure status. The following V2 updates will still be processed as normal.

More than one update work process will be present in an R/3 system.

The dispatcher

The dispatcher is the interface between the SAPGUI and all work processes. It assigns processing requests from all users to the various work processes and returns the results to the proper recipient. It also accepts requests from dispatchers in other application servers. In this case a message server (see below) handles the communication between dispatchers. Figure 2.3 illustrates this architecture. The dispatcher also sets priorities for update processes, handles all data requests that are not handled by the RDBMS and works very closely with the operating system.

There is only one dispatcher per application server.

The message server

Figure 2.3 shows an example of a distributed R/3 system consisting of two dialog servers, a batch server and a database server. In this type of architecture a message server is required to coordinate the activities for all application servers and to pass messages to the appropriate dispatcher. The types of messages that are exchanged between the application servers are normally update triggers, batch job triggers, enqueue/dequeue requests and exchanges of tasks.

Only one message server can exist in a given R/3 system.

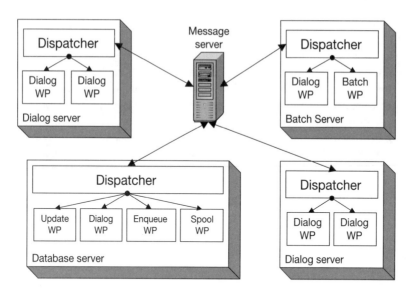

Figure 2.3   R/3 distributed architecture

The SAP gateway server

For completeness it is worth mentioning that multiple R/3 systems, and therefore multiple database servers, can be linked together via an SAP gateway server (more commonly known as the CPIC server). This server can handle communication between multiple R/3 systems, a mixture of R/3 and R/2 systems as well as external non-SAP applications.

If you are responsible for multiple R/3 systems they may be linked via a CPIC server. For backup and recovery purposes each database server should be backed up and recovered independently.

The database server

A typical database server will consist of at least one dialog work process, several update work processes, an enqueue work process and a spool work process. Update work processes are normally executed on the database server to shorten the communication path to the database and therefore improve performance. The directory structure and general architecture of Oracle as configured to support R/3 systems will be discussed in the next chapter.

In an R/3 system the database includes program source code, screen layouts, text items, menu options, printer definitions, statistical information and, of course, the application data itself. This is why it is vitally important that the database is protected at all costs, making a sound backup/recovery strategy all the more important.

2.2   System interfaces

There are four main interfaces in an SAP R/3 system. They are:

- the operating system interface
- the database interface
- the presentation interface
- the communications interface (this interface is present in the other three and is outside the scope of this book so will not be discussed).

2.2.1   The operating system interface

SAP R/3 runs on many different platforms and operating systems. In order for the system to operate identically on all of these platforms, SAP developed the Basis system. This system provides a set of common services that isolate R/3 from the underlying operating system. The types of services supplied are message handling, memory management, scheduling and several other services which could be partially done by the operating system but R/3 executes them internally for performance reasons and for portability.

2.2.2   The database interface

In a similar fashion to the operating system interface, the database interface isolates R/3 from the different databases supported by SAP. The main task of this interface is to convert the SQL requests from the ABAP/4 programs into requests understood by the underlying database. The interface also performs syntax checks on the SQL and has some intelligence built into it which tries to optimize the use (or reuse) of the R/3 buffers where the same SQL statement may be run multiple times. These buffers are held locally in the memory of each application server.

2.2.3   The presentation interface

The presentation interface, commonly known as the SAPGUI, is the interface the user uses to communicate with the R/3 system. All of the elements of the interface, including the menu options, buttons etc. are stored in the database. This allows SAP to use an identical interface irrespective of the system R/3 is installed on.

2.3   Memory management

To maintain the performance and reliability of an R/3 system it is important to understand how memory is managed. Starting with release 3.0, SAP introduced a new method of memory management, which improved the performance and reliability of the R/3 system.

As discussed earlier, it is possible for more than one work process to perform tasks for a single user. The dispatcher handles this sharing of tasks across several work processes. Each work process requires access to user context information such as authorizations, field information, internal tables and so on. In prior releases this information was held in a roll file on disk and paged in and out of the work process local memory area. This involved copying the roll data from one work process to another. In release 3.0 upward this information is held in a shared memory area and R/3 simply changes the pointers to that area for each work process. The amount of memory required by the context information can be dynamically extended (previously the amount of context was limited to the maximum size of the roll file).

R/3, and not the operating system, handles most of the memory management tasks to keep the R/3 system portable across different operating system types. For more detailed information please refer to the SAP R/3 manuals.

2.4   Putting it all together – the R/3 instance

To complete our overview of the SAP R/3 architecture we need to define the concept of an instance. If you have experience of the Oracle RDBMS you will have already come across the term 'instance' which, in Oracle terms, refers to the Oracle shared memory area, all data files, control files and redo logs, together with the background processes. SAP architected R/3 along the same guidelines.

An R/3 instance is a logical grouping of services which are:

- administered together

- started and stopped simultaneously

- identified by a single name.

It is possible to have a central R/3 instance where all of the possible services (dialog, update, enqueue, batch, spool and message server processes) are installed on a single computer. In a more typical R/3 installation these services are spread amongst several computers with some acting purely as dialog servers, batch servers and database servers. In this configuration there are several instances which cooperate with one another (see Figure 2.3).

It is possible to have more than one R/3 instance on a single machine providing there is sufficient memory and disk space to accommodate them. This type of configuration is rare in a production R/3 system.

2.5   R/3 transactions – introducing the Logical Unit of Work (LUW)

Should a failure occur somewhere in an R/3 system it is important for you, the DBA, to determine where the problem lies and to investigate the current state of the database

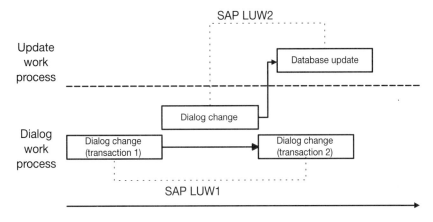

SAP LUW1 is interrupted by LUW2 causing LUW1 to be
processed as two transactions

Figure 2.4   SAP Logical Unit of Work (LUW)

before deciding which method of recovery to perform (we shall discuss recovery in more
depth later). To be able to investigate potential causes of failure it is essential to understand the concept of a Logical Unit of Work (LUW), as defined by SAP, and to also
understand how this concept is implemented within the definition of an R/3 transaction.

Conceptually, a Logical Unit of Work (LUW) is a locking mechanism that protects the
integrity of an R/3 transaction. An LUW is a set of steps within a transaction, all of which
must either be completed successfully or, if there are errors, must all be undone. Figure 2.4
illustrates an R/3 LUW.

An ABAP/4 COMMIT WORK or a database COMMIT, whichever occurs sooner,
defines the end of an LUW and the beginning of the next one. As can be seen from Figure
2.4, an LUW can contain several transactions. However should this LUW fail after, for
example, the first database COMMIT then the LUW will only be undone (rolled back) as
far as the previous database commit.

In ABAP/4 LUWs can be nested within one another and they can be executed by various work processes, especially if the LUW contains many dialog steps. To avoid too much
complexity and to help the DBA unravel a transaction if it fails, SAP recommends that an
LUW does not contain more than 5–10 dialog steps. Also in release 3.0 upward it is possible to allocate a single work process exclusively to an LUW.

2.6   Backup and recovery tools for R/3

In this section we will take our first look at the backup and recovery tools available for
SAP R/3. Throughout the remainder of the book we will include examples of backup and
recovery using both the SAP supplied tools and the Oracle backup tools supplied with
Oracle7 and Oracle8.

2.6.1   Tools supplied by SAP

R/3 is shipped with three utilities: BRBACKUP, which is the backup utility used by the SAPDBA program; BRARCHIVE, which is used to backup the Oracle archived redo logs; and BRRESTORE, which is used to restore the database files, control files, online redo logs and/or archived redo logs back to a consistent state.

When determining how to backup an R/3 system the DBA has several choices. The SAPDBA program, supplied with R/3, can be used. This acts as an interface to the BRBACKUP, BRARCHIVE and BRRESTORE command line utilities. Alternatively the Oracle-supplied backup tools can be used to backup the relevant database files. These tools would be executed externally to the R/3 system and therefore no information about the backups that had been performed would be available from within R/3. The final option is for the DBA to use some backup/recovery tool supplied by a third-party software vendor. Such tools can use the BACKINT interface which is a backup API (application programming interface) defined by SAP specifically to allow third-party backup solutions to integrate fully with the R/3 environment. Tools that use this interface are certified by SAP for use with R/3 and are capable of reporting details of backups back to the R/3 system which can then be viewed within CCMS (Computing Center Management System).

Let's look at each of the SAP supplied utilities in more detail. Figure 2.5 shows the R/3 backup/recovery architecture.

BRBACKUP

BRBACKUP allows online or offline backups to be taken of Oracle control files, data files and online redo logs. The program can either be run from the command line or via the

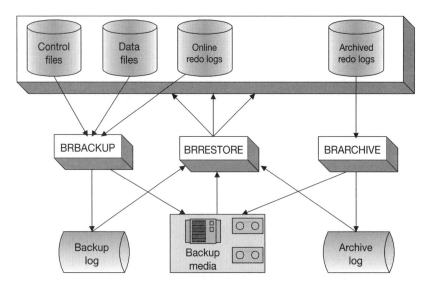

Figure 2.5   R/3 backup/recovery architecture

SAPDBA interface. As well as the actual backup, the program performs additional functions necessary to complete its job as follows:

- it will automatically change the state of the database depending on whether the backup is to be run online or offline;

- checks the status of all files;

- optimizes the distribution of the data on the backup media; and

- will compress the data if required.

It is also possible to include non-database files in the backup. These types of files would include programs, SAP profiles, SAP logs etc.; in fact any directory can be included in the backup.

BRBACKUP supports Oracle raw devices and parallel server configurations.

BRARCHIVE

BRARCHIVE is used to backup the Oracle archived redo logs. R/3 requires that Oracle be run in ARCHIVELOG mode. This means that when Oracle has filled an online redo log it will automatically copy it (archive) to another directory. It is these archive copies that BRARCHIVE backs up.

SAP requires ARCHIVELOG mode for the following reasons:

- a consistent database status can only be recovered if all the relevant redo logs are available;

- a recovery to a point-in-time can only be achieved if the redo logs are archived.

Because of the importance of the archived redo logs, BRARCHIVE can write more than one duplicate copy of each redo log to a backup device – this duplication can be performed in parallel. BRARCHIVE automatically deletes redo logs that have been backed up. This is to ensure that no problems are introduced due to the archive log directory filling up and stopping the database. Archived redo logs can be copied to tape or disk; it is recommended that you backup the logs to disk in the first instance and then to tape.

By keeping copies of the logs on disk you will be able to perform a faster recovery. Most of the time spent recovering a database is taken up by restoring the required archived logs from tape to disk.

BRRESTORE

BRRESTORE is the utility used to restore database data files, control files, online or offline redo logs and any other files backed up with BRBACKUP.

It is possible to specify individual files, tablespaces, complete backups or the sequence numbers of redo log files to restore. The program will automatically determine which tape is required and whether there is sufficient free disk space to restore the requested object.

2.6.2   Tools supplied by Oracle

The version of Oracle you are using with R/3 will determine which backup/recovery utility is available to you.

With Oracle7 backup and recovery is performed using Oracle Enterprise Manager (OEM) which is a Graphical User Interface (GUI) that is designed to make backups of Oracle data files easier. The product contains tape management facilities and allows online backups to be performed. The tool will create backup scripts via a wizard to allow the DBA to backup all data files associated with a particular tablespace. The same tool is used to recover data files and to manage redo log files.

With Oracle8 comes a new tool called Recovery Manager (RMAN). As mentioned earlier, a large number of the severity 1 database down problems were prolonged by the inexperienced DBA being unaware of the correct recovery procedure for the type of failure the database suffered. To help with this situation, Recovery Manager has been provided. Recovery Manager is simply a tool that allows a DBA to regularly backup and, when needed, recover database objects via a command line. It is also possible to use the tool via the Oracle Enterprise Manager interface. When used this way the OEM GUI simply builds the command line parameters required to run RMAN, and executes them. This saves the DBA from having to learn all of the command line options in RMAN.

RMAN differs from the Oracle7 OEM method of backups in that it stores details of all backups in a backup catalog which is simply a set of tables stored in an Oracle database somewhere, preferably separate from the database being backed up. This catalog is used by RMAN to determine what needs backing up, and what tapes contain the required files for recovery purposes. In previous releases the DBA had to determine this.

If these tools are used instead of the SAP supplied utilities, they execute externally to the R/3 system and do not interface to it. Therefore any records of backups or recoveries that have been performed on your R/3 system this way are not made available from within CCMS. However, from release 4.5A of R/3 SAP have incorporated the use of RMAN into SAPDBA, which will perform the backup and recovery functions. If you perform your backups and recoveries via SAPDBA, then they will be recorded within the R/3 backup and recovery logs and viewable through CCMS.

2.6.3   Tools supplied by third-party software vendors

At the time of writing this book there are 25 backup and recovery products certified to run within the SAP R/3 environment, with several more currently going through the SAP certification process. The SAP Certification and Validation Centre puts all third-party tools, which fully use the BACKINT interface to R/3, through a certification process. This ensures that each tool correctly uses the interface and therefore the customer can be assured that each solution is integrated with R/3 to the satisfaction of SAP.

Throughout this book we use examples of backup and recovery procedures using both SAPDBA and the Oracle backup/recovery tools in both Oracle7 and Oracle8.

To obtain a full list of SAP backup and recovery solutions partners please visit the SAP website at *http://www.sap.com/products/compsoft/certify/index.htm*.

3 Oracle architecture

Before we can begin to plan our backup/recovery strategy for our SAP R/3 system, and successfully implement it, we need to understand the Oracle architecture – both from the viewpoint of what gets installed where and what is and is not important. This section will explain the various Oracle objects, with which you must be familiar, together with how Oracle works. In later chapters we will discuss how your backup and recovery strategy is affected by the requirements of the SAP R/3 environment.

3.1 The Oracle architecture under R/3

3.1.1 Directory structure

The Oracle RDBMS is installed as part of the R/3 installation. When it is installed several subdirectories are created underneath the directory pointed to by the ORACLE_HOME environment variable. The top level directory in an SAP installation is normally `/oracle/<SID>` (SID being the SAP system name which in a single Oracle instance install is normally the same as the Oracle SID). The subdirectories found within this top level directory are:

- `/oracle/<SID>/sapdata<n>` – the identifier <n> is a number from 1 to the number of directories required to hold all of the tablespaces containing the R/3 data. Under normal conditions there will be 5 or 6 of these directories.

- `/oracle/<SID>/origlogA` – contains the master redo logs in the first redo log group.

- `/oracle/<SID>/origlogB` – contains the master redo logs in the second redo log group.

- `/oracle/<SID>/mirrorlogA` – contains the mirrored redo logs in the first redo log group.

- `/oracle/<SID>/mirrorlogB` – contains the mirrored redo logs in the second redo log group.

- `/oracle/<SID>/saparch` – contains the archived (offline) redo logs.

- `/oracle/<SID>/sapreorg` – a work area for performing database reorganizations and any other maintenance tasks required on the database.

- `/oracle/<SID>/sapcheck` – log and analysis files generated from the SAPDBA utility.

- `/oracle/<SID>/sapbackup` – contains the log file output from backups run using SAPDBA. Other directories may exist in here containing backups performed to disk.

- `/oracle/<SID>/saptrace` – Oracle trace files created by the background and user processes together with the Oracle alert log.

- `/oracle/<SID>/dbs` – this directory holds the Oracle initialization file, a mirrored copy of the Oracle control file, parameter files for SAPDBA and the BRBACKUP utility as well as the SAPDBA help text files.

- `/oracle/<SID>/bin` – the directory containing the Oracle executables.

- `/oracle/<SID>/network` – contains several subdirectories which hold various files for the control and configuration of the Oracle communications program SQL*Net (or Net8 as it is now called when shipped with Oracle8).

- `Other directories` – there are several other directories which form part of the Oracle RDBMS installation which mainly contain message files for the various programs and utilities.

A similar directory structure exists whether you are running Oracle on Microsoft Windows NT, UNIX or some other type of operating system. All of our examples will reference the UNIX environment.

3.1.2   The Oracle SGA and background processes

In order for Oracle to function it requires access to several memory areas, collectively known as the System Global Area (SGA), together with a set of background processes that perform certain specific tasks. Together these background processes and memory areas are known as an **Oracle Instance**.

The SGA is particularly important for the overall performance of Oracle, and hence your R/3 system. It consists of two parts: a fixed size part containing information about the Oracle instance and other data used by the background processes; and a variable size part that holds various buffers used for the caching of data, SQL statements, locks etc. The latter is the part that is tunable by the DBA. The size of these buffers is determined by various parameters found in the initialization file `init<SID>.ora` (see later in this chapter for a brief discussion of this file) which is read by Oracle when the database is started.

The parameters the DBA should be most concerned with when tuning Oracle with SAP R/3 are the following:

- `db_block_size` – which specifies the size of each Oracle block in bytes. In an R/3 system the Oracle block size is normally 8K and is not usually changed.

- `db_block_buffers` – is the total number of data buffers to be stored in the SGA. The value of this parameter multiplied by the Oracle block size determines the total size, in bytes, of the buffer cache.

- `shared_pool_size` – this area caches the SQL statements shared by several processes. The parameter specifies the total size of this cache in bytes.

- `log_buffers` – this parameter determines the size of the buffer that holds data to be written to the online redo logs. When this buffer becomes full the contents will be flushed to the latest open online redo log. Making this buffer too small will cause frequent writes to the redo logs, slowing down performance, too large and you are at risk of losing some redo data.

The background processes are responsible for executing many different tasks. They are permanently running in the background and are started as part of the database startup procedure. Do not confuse Oracle background processes with user (or server) processes. User processes are responsible for executing user applications and perform tasks on behalf of user requests. Background processes, on the other hand, execute functions on behalf of the Oracle database kernel and are essential to the correct operation of the database system.

All of the Oracle background processes are named according to their specific function. The type and number of these processes varies depending on the Oracle configuration you are running. In a standard R/3 installation you will see the following background processes:

- `DBWR` (Database Writer) – this process is responsible for writing the contents of the db_block_buffers in the SGA to the various tablespace data files (or raw devices) on disk. This process will only write data when instructed to do so by other processes or when the db_block_buffers cache is full. This prevents excessive physical disk writes, which can hinder performance.

- `LGWR` (Log Writer) – this process writes the contents of the log_buffer to the current open online redo log file(s) on disk. More than one log file may be written to if you have configured Oracle to write to multiple redo log groups or if you are duplexing the redo logs in Oracle8. The log writer will also update the headers of the control files and data files with the latest checkpoint information (unless the `CKPT` background process is running).

- `CKPT` (Checkpoint) – this process updates the control file and data file headers with the latest checkpoint information. This process is not started by default, the DBA must request it to be started by setting the parameter `CHECKPOINT_PROCESS` to true in the `init<SID>.ora` file. In most R/3 installations it is not necessary to start this additional process, the `LGWR` process can handle the writing of checkpoint information. The only time this process needs to be enabled is if there are a very large number of data files and the checkpoint process is degrading overall system response times. Checkpoints occur when an online redo log file fills and Oracle switches to the next one, or at a predefined interval determined by the `LOG_CHECKPOINT_INTERVAL` parameter in the `init<SID>.ora`.

- `SMON` (System Monitor) – this process is responsible for cleaning up after abnormal behaviour. It recovers the database after a crash, when Oracle is restarted, by rolling back transactions that were not processed prior to the crash. It will also clean up temporary segments that are no longer being used by Oracle; these segments are usually stored in the `TEMP` tablespace (or the tablespace allocated for this purpose by the DBA). `SMON` is also responsible for coalescing contiguous free space.

- PMON (Process Monitor) – this process recovers and releases resources used by abnormally terminated user processes. PMON will release any locks the user process was holding at the time of the termination.

- ARCH (Archiver) – this process will copy the online redo logs to the archive redo log area. When a redo log fills, a checkpoint occurs, a new online redo log is opened, and the recently filled redo log is archived by this process. This process is only started when the ARCHIVELOG mode is set, which is the default on all R/3 systems. By setting this parameter you are able to perform point-in-time recovery of your R/3 system.

Other processes you may see on your system are as follows:

- RECO (Recoverer) – this process is only seen in a distributed database environment. It is responsible for recovering distributed in-doubt transactions i.e. transactions that were unable to complete due to some failure.

- LCK (Lock) – is only seen in a parallel server implementation. The Oracle Parallel Server (OPS) option consists of multiple Oracle instances. This process provides a locking mechanism across those instances. There can be up to ten such processes, named LCK0 – LCK9. In most cases one such process is sufficient.

- SNP (Snapshot Refresh) – this process updates table snapshots in a distributed database environment. There can be up to eleven such processes, named SNP0 – SNP10, which will share the responsibility of automatically updating the snapshots.

- D (Dispatcher) – the dispatcher allows multiple user processes to share one server process. This background process is found in a multi-threaded server (MTS) environment. There may be several of these identified as Dnnn where nnn represents a number.

3.1.3   Important files

The important files to note when considering your backup policy are the control files, data files, online and archive redo logs, the initialization file, and the Oracle software. A full operating system backup will include all of these objects and more but there will be times when it will be necessary to perform a partial backup of some of these objects – it is then that you will need to determine what needs to be backed up and when. Hopefully this book will be able to answer these and many other questions for you.

Let's begin by looking at each of the important files in turn, starting with the control files.

Control files

The control file is one of the most important database files. Oracle uses this file to store information about:

- what tablespaces are contained within your database;

- what data files you have, where they are located and what their state is;

- the name, location and status of your online redo logs;

- the System Change Numbers (SCN) which Oracle uses for recovery purposes (SCNs will be explained later);

- information on the backups you have performed with Oracle Recovery Manager (RMAN).

It is essential that you have at least three copies of your control file on different disks and different disk controllers. Oracle maintains all copies of the control files automatically and locates each copy by reading the CONTROL_FILES parameter in the init<SID>.ora initialization file. These files must be backed up regularly; they can be backed up online as we shall discuss later. Should you lose your control file it is possible for Oracle to recreate it but this will involve the database being down. SAP includes the relevant parameter in the init<SID>.ora file to mirror your control file in three different places. By default the directories where your control file and mirror copies will be stored are:

- /oracle/<SID>/dbs

- /oracle/<SID>/sapdata1/cntrl

- /oracle/<SID>/sapdata2/cntrl.

If you wish to create more control files, simply add their path and filename to the CONTROL_FILES parameter. Remember to make sure that all control files are on different physical disks, and preferably different disk controllers for added security.

Data files

The data files are where Oracle stores your data and they are logically grouped into tablespaces. A data file can belong to one and only one tablespace; each tablespace may have many data files. When Oracle is installed a tablespace called SYSTEM is created where all of the internal data dictionary objects are stored. Other tablespaces will also be created such as USER, ROLLBACK, TEMPORARY, TOOLS and so on. If a tablespace runs out of space Oracle will report an error. If this occurs frequently it is necessary to investigate the reasons why. It may be due to database objects such as tables growing more rapidly than was originally anticipated, alternatively it may be down to an inefficient allocation of storage space. In these cases the fundamental problem should be fixed. In emergencies the DBA may add another data file to the tablespace until a more permanent resolution is implemented. Over time the number of data files a tablespace contains may grow. This means that the backup requirements for those tablespaces also change, something that has to be considered every time a data file is added. This is also true when the DBA adds new tablespaces to the database.

Redo logs

The redo logs contain a record of all changes made to the data in your database. These data files are updated by the Oracle Log Writer process (LGWR) and are commonly known as the online redo logs. Offline redo logs are copies of the online logs that have been archived to a different destination by the Oracle Archiver (ARCH) background process.

This process will only be performing the archiving function if the database is running in ARCHIVELOG mode, which should always be the case in an R/3 installation (see later for a further discussion of this). It is important to protect the archived redo logs from failure as Oracle will use these to recover in the event of data loss. The online redo logs are also used to perform crash recovery when the Oracle database is restarted after a crash.

For extra fault tolerance, Oracle can multiplex the redo logs (in other words mirror them) so that should one log fail the mirror copy can be used. It is also possible now with Oracle8 to duplex the archived log files. This means Oracle will maintain more than one copy of each archive log – the number of copies kept is controlled by the LOG_ARCHIVE_MIN_SUCCEED_DEST parameter in the init<SID>.ora file.

The standard R/3 installation creates four redo log files of 20MB each stored in two directories /oracle/<SID>/origlogA and /oracle/<SID>/origlogB. Each directory contains the original redo log and a mirror copy of that log is held in a separate directory /oracle/<SID>/mirrorlogA and /oracle/<SID>/mirrorlogB. You must make sure that the mirror copy is located on a different physical disk (and different disk controller) from the original. If you are using RAID devices it is a good idea to locate your redo logs on RAID-1 where the disk controller will automatically handle the mirroring of these files for you. The mirroring of your redo logs is strongly recommended by SAP.

The initialization file

When Oracle is started it reads an initialization file known by DBAs as the INIT.ORA file. This file is actually named init<SID>.ora, the <SID> being the name of your database. This file contains a large number of parameters that determine, for example, how large the System Global Area (SGA) should be and, therefore, how much memory Oracle will use, where the control files are located and various other important facts required to start and run the database. Like the control file, the initialization file is essential to Oracle's operation and therefore should be backed up regularly. In fact it would make sense to keep more than one copy online in case of accidental deletion although if you make any changes to the file you must remember to change all copies to keep them in line.

Trace files and Oracle alert file

When we described the Oracle directory structure as installed with SAP R/3 we briefly described the location of the R/3 trace files stored in /oracle/<SID>/saptrace. These trace files hold information used for problem diagnosis, and are placed in one of two sub-directories within the saptrace directory: background and usertrace. Usertrace contains trace files created by user processes. Oracle creates these when a process experiences a problem or terminates abnormally. The background directory holds the trace files created by the Oracle background processes, and also contains the Oracle alert file, which is named as alert_<SID>.log.

The alert file is a good starting place for a DBA who has to diagnose database and/or process failures. Before performing a recovery it is good practice to consult this file to determine the cause of failure and find out any information associated with other processes executing at the time the problem occurred. This information, together with information from other trace files, can be used to determine the possible cause of the failure and therefore the type of recovery that needs to be performed.

The alert file contains details of all database activity, such as database startup and shutdown, the parameters in effect, the activities of the various Oracle background processes, redo log switches, tablespace modifications, error messages, names of trace files created by user processes and information on backups. This file is continuously appended to and for this reason it is good practice to monitor the growth of this file and periodically delete it. If the alert file is deleted, Oracle will create another one the next time it needs to write to it – this will not affect the performance of the database in any way. Some DBAs will take a copy of the alert file before deleting it so that they have a history of all database activity over time. SAP does not provide any tools for managing the Oracle alert file.

As well as the alert file and trace files created by Oracle, the R/3 system offers a variety of diagnostic tools the DBA can use for problem investigation. One of these diagnostic tools is the ability to trace a number of operations including tracing all SQL activity, ABAP/4 programs and internal operations of the R/3 system (known as developer traces).

The Oracle log modes

Oracle can be run in two modes: ARCHIVELOG and NOARCHIVELOG. The mode you use determines whether the online redo logs will automatically be archived (ARCHIVELOG mode) when they become full. Archiving in this sense means making a copy of the online redo log at another location. SAP and Oracle strongly recommend running the database in ARCHIVELOG mode with R/3. This gives the DBA more recovery options in the event of something going wrong and allows point-in-time recovery to be performed, if required, together with logical database recoveries.

In order for the ARCHIVELOG mode to be active, two parameters must be set in the init<SID>.ora file: log_archive_start = true and log_archive_dest which points to the directory where the archive redo logs are to be written. By default R/3 sets this parameter to /oracle/<SID>/saparch/<SID>arch. The last part of this parameter, <SID>arch, is used by Oracle as the prefix for the filename which will also have a sequence number added to it. Oracle will also add the file extension .dbf to the end of the filename.

It is vital to have enough disk space to store the archived redo logs. If Oracle runs out of space the ARCH background process will stop and so will the database. It is important, therefore, to monitor the directory where these files are being written, to periodically back them up to tape and delete them. The BRARCHIVE utility is provided by SAP for this purpose. If you are not short of disk space it is still wise to backup the archive redo logs but NOT delete them. Recovery will be faster if the required archive redo logs are on disk. Most of the recovery time is taken with waiting for the archive redo logs to be read from tape.

From time to time you may need to disable ARCHIVELOG mode. In fact SAP recommends that you disable this mode before performing a long running reorganization such as a full database or large tablespace reorganization. This avoids filling up the archive log directory and therefore stopping the database. There are several ways to switch log modes:

- manually using the ALTER   DATABASE   ARCHIVELOG or ALTER   DATABASE NOARCHIVELOG commands in the Oracle Server Manager product;

- using the DB-TOOL option within the R3INST installation tool;

- within SAPDBA by selecting option *f – Archive mode* from the initial menu.

Whichever method is used the R/3 instance must be stopped and the database closed. SAPDBA will perform both of these actions when you request a change of mode.

After the reorganization is finished a full backup is mandatory and ARCHIVELOG mode must be enabled once again.

The Oracle software

As discussed earlier, when Oracle is installed various directories are created to house the executable code, function libraries and so on. There are also several SQL script files that are essential when installing or reinstalling the database system. The code and associated files should be backed up after initial installation. They will then only need to be backed up again if any software patches are applied which may change one or more executables, or when you install an Oracle upgrade.

It is good practice to keep your Oracle software backup separate from data backups and to keep a copy of the software off site, possibly at a disaster recovery centre.

The concepts we have discussed are illustrated in Figure 3.1. This diagram also shows how these components interact within the Oracle architecture.

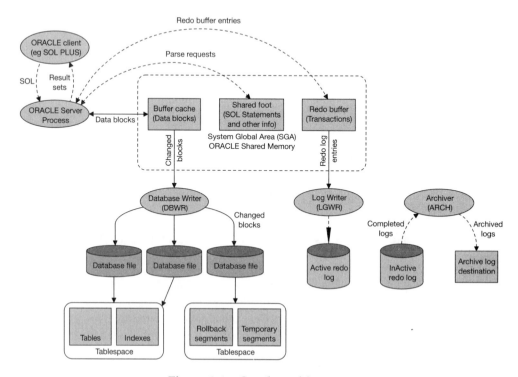

Figure 3.1   Oracle architecture

3.2   New features in Oracle

Ever since Oracle7 was released, Oracle Corporation have been enhancing their database management system with new features covering everything from enhancing PL/SQL for programmers through to adding more parallel options to support increasing numbers of users. In this section we take a look at those options Oracle have included in versions 7.1, 7.2, 7.3 and Oracle8 which affect your backup and recovery strategy. Other features and functions introduced in these releases are not covered.

3.2.1   Oracle7 release 7.1

The features we will look at here are:

- symmetric replication
- consistent snapshot refresh
- read-only tablespaces
- parallel recovery.

Symmetric replication

This feature was introduced by Oracle to allow updatable copies of data to reside at multiple sites in a distributed database environment. This means that when a row, or several rows, are changed in a table those changes will automatically be replicated to all sites that also contain that table. Problems can arise if the same row is updated at more than one site at the same time. Oracle has to work out how those conflicts are resolved by providing conflict-resolution routines. It is also possible for the DBA to write his/her own routines for this purpose.

From a backup and recovery point of view it is necessary for the DBA to understand how symmetric replication works in order to be able to recover a database, or databases, that are part of the replication architecture.

Consistent snapshot refresh

Snapshots were made available in Oracle7 and are another mechanism for replicating data across databases using the Oracle Distributed Option. There are two ways in which the data for a table can be updated via a snapshot. A *simple snapshot* uses a snapshot log to send just the transactions that need to be applied to the table. This reduces the amount of data going over the network. Oracle can only use this mechanism if the replication is a one-to-one replication, i.e. from one table on the master database to one table on the remote database – hence the term 'simple'. A *complex snapshot* performs a complete refresh of the table and therefore does not use the logs. A snapshot is complex when two or more tables are joined and the results are used to update a single table on the remote database.

In release 7.1 Oracle introduced the concept of a *snapshot group*. This allows two or more snapshots in a parent–child relationship to be treated as a single snapshot for update purposes. When the update is applied all shapshots in the group will be updated.

Read-only tablespaces

Many applications use tables that are only ever read and not updated. Such tables are usually found in Data Warehouses but can also be found in many other types of applications. The read-only tablespace is ideal for these types of tables.

When a tablespace is set to read-only mode all the data files that belong to the tablespace are also marked as read-only in the control file. During database backups these tablespaces only need to be backed up the first time they are created and populated with data (after making them read-only), they do not then need to be backed up again. Read-only tablespaces can be brought on and off-line in exactly the same way as read-write tablespaces. When an Oracle database crashes, Oracle will perform automatic recovery when it is restarted. Oracle will ignore read-only tablespaces during the recovery process because no redo needs to be applied to these tablespaces. This can improve the speed with which Oracle becomes available again after a crash. We will discuss read-only tablespaces in more detail later.

In order for a tablespace to be set as read-only, several criteria need to be satisfied:

- the `init<SID>.ora` parameter COMPATIBLE needs to be set to 7.1.0;

- the tablespace must be online;

- there should be no rollback statements in the tablespace;

- the tablespace must not be in hot backup mode, i.e. the ALTER TABLESPACE <tablespace name> BEGIN BACKUP must not have been executed against the tablespace;

- there should be no active transactions in the database.

Parallel recovery

The time it takes to recover a database after a crash is critical for high availability databases. Parallel recovery provides the ability to use multiple recovery threads on multi-CPU systems. The number of threads used for any recovery is determined by the `init<SID>.ora` parameter RECOVERY_PARALLELISM and these processes will be shared across multiple instances if you are using the Oracle Parallel Server. It is also possible to override the `init<SID>.ora` parameter when using the RECOVER DATABASE, RECOVER TABLESPACE, or RECOVER DATAFILE commands. For example, RECOVER DATABASE PARALLEL DEGREE 3 INSTANCE 2; will use three recovery threads applying redo concurrently. We have specified two instances making a total of six recovery threads, three per instance.

The processes are coordinated by a master process which reads each redo entry in turn from the redo logs and passes the change information (known as change vectors) to the relevant slave process. The slave process reads the data blocks to be changed into the SGA and then applies the changes. The master process guarantees to pass all changes made to the same data block to the same slave process to ensure that the changes are applied in the correct order.

The optimal number of recovery threads to use depends on whether the operating system you are running Oracle on supports asynchronous I/O. If your machine does not support asynchronous I/O, it is usual to have between four to six threads per CPU; on asynchronous architectures one to two threads is sufficient.

3.2.2   Oracle7 release 7.2

Data corruption detection

In release 7.2 a checksum feature was added which allows early detection of corruption in either the redo logs or data blocks. New `init<SID>.ora` parameters were added to control the switching on and off of these checks. When `LOG_BLOCK_CHECKSUM` is set to TRUE redo block corruption will be detected during archiving or recovery. You also need to set the `COMPATIBLE` parameter equal to 7.2.0 or higher. When `DB_BLOCK_CHECKSUM` is set to TRUE Oracle will calculate the checksum for each data block it reads into the SGA and store it in the block header. The next time the block is read this checksum will be recalculated and compared to the value in the block header. This parameter was available in earlier releases of Oracle but was not documented. **It is important to note that these parameters should only be used on advice from Oracle customer support**.

Improvement in crash recovery

To improve the time it takes to recover the database in the event of a crash, Oracle allowed the command `ALTER DATABASE DATAFILE <data file name> END BACKUP` to be executed whilst the database is mounted but not open. In previous releases this statement could only be used on an open database. The reason Oracle did this was to get around the following problem. If the database crashes whilst an online backup of a tablespace is taking place, Oracle detects that media recovery is required when the database is restarted. Depending on the amount of activity on the database at the time of the crash and hence the amount of redo generated, it can take a long time for Oracle to become available again. It is not necessary for Oracle to have to perform a full media recovery on the tablespace being backed up because any changes to the data files for the tablespace will have been updated. Therefore all Oracle needs to do is to update the data file header. The contents of the data file will be correct and we will discuss the reasons why when we look at how Oracle uses the System Change Number (SCN) to detect and perform recovery. To avoid redo being applied to all the data files in the tablespace the `ALTER DATABASE END BACKUP` command should be issued before the database is opened. This will force Oracle to update the file headers avoiding the need to perform media recovery and therefore improving the length of time it takes for Oracle to restart.

3.2.3   Oracle7 release 7.3

This release provided significant backup and recovery improvements including:

- fast rollback of transactions
- new views for media recovery
- hot standby databases.

Fast transaction rollback

When Oracle performs a recovery it does so in two stages. First it rolls forward applying all redo records to the appropriate data blocks then it rolls back by applying redo from the rollback segments for those transactions that had not committed. Oracle is then made available for users to access.

Release 7.3 introduced a fast transaction rollback feature to improve the performance of transaction recovery. Now when Oracle is restarted after a crash it performs a roll forward as before. When the roll forward is complete, it then makes the database available to users after which it will perform transaction recovery.

To be able to do this, Oracle changed the behaviour of the PMON background process. Before release 7.3, PMON used to perform recovery serially and always completely recovered a transaction before moving onto the next. Since release 7.3, PMON, as well as foreground processes, now perform recovery in a cyclic fashion and in parallel. This is how it works.

After the database is opened, PMON scans the dictionary table UNDO$ to find transactions that need recovery, it then applies a small number of redo entries to the database, i.e. it performs a partial recovery for each transaction. It keeps doing this for each transaction in turn until all redo has been applied for all transactions. If a transaction that is running on the database, whilst recovery is taking place, needs a row that is locked by a transaction that has yet to be rolled back, the foreground process requiring the row will recover the transaction itself so that it can continue. This foreground process will also perform a partial recovery on the rest of the rollback segment.

Because transaction recovery is taking place whilst the database is open and in use, Oracle has to ensure that suspect rows do not cause problems. Oracle achieves this by keeping the row-level locks that the suspect transactions held before the crash and only releasing them when the transaction has been successfully rolled back.

New views for media recovery

Two new views were provided to allow the DBA to monitor the database recovery process. These views are held in the Program Global Area (PGA) within the Oracle SGA and destroyed once recovery is complete.

V$RECOVERY_FILE_STATUS shows the status of each data file in the database. The STATUS column can have the following values:

- *Current* – meaning the data file does not need recovery.
- *In recovery* – meaning that the data file is being recovered.

- *Not recovered* – meaning that the data file will not be recovered because it was offline at the time recovery was started. It is important to remember that offline data files will not be recovered by the recover database command. You should check for data files with a status of 'Not recovered' before opening the database with the RESETLOGS option, otherwise you may find that when the data file is brought back online it needs recovery but the redo data has been destroyed by the RESETLOGS!

V$RECOVERY_STATUS shows statistics for the current recovery process. It includes the point-in-time to which the recovery has occurred, the redo thread currently being applied, the redo log sequence number needed for recovery, the file name and status of the previous redo log that was applied. When the recovery process returns control to the user you can query this view to see why.

The REASON column provides this information and can contain one of the following values:

- NEED LOG – requires the name of the next redo log to apply.

- LOG REUSED – the redo log needed was overwritten so the archive redo log is required instead.

- THREAD DISABLED – the current recovery thread was disabled at this point-in-time.

Once recovery is completed this view will return zero rows.

Hot standby database

Disaster recovery planning and implementation has always been a 'disaster' with Oracle. In release 7.3 this was addressed with the ability to implement a hot standby database and to maintain that database by applying the archive redo logs from the production system. Whilst this appears attractive, currently it is difficult to maintain, implement and monitor and there are plenty of places where problems can occur. We will discuss these later and suggest some ways in which you can provide yourself with a suitable insurance policy against such problems. Despite the difficulties, it is still worth persevering with the implementation of a hot standby database in situations where it is essential to have a disaster recovery policy.

The hot standby database feature involves implementing an *exact* copy of the production system. This includes using the same version of Oracle and preferably the same version of the operating system as well. I say 'preferably' because Oracle does not require you to have exactly the same version of the operating system (or even the same operating system!). However if you do have a different operating system, or different version of the same operating system, it increases the administration headache and it is harder to rectify problems when they occur.

The standby database is always mounted and in recovery mode. When a new redo log is archived the archive copy is transferred to the machine containing the standby database and applied using some new commands created for this purpose. When the production database fails the DBA can activate the standby database.

For a complete discussion on planning, designing and implementing this feature please refer to Chapter 7 – Disaster Recovery.

3.2.4   Oracle8

Oracle8 is a major new release of the RDBMS that contains many new features. Here we will discuss the following that are within the scope of this book:

- partitioning
- the new ROWID format
- Recovery Manager.

Partitioning

Partitioning provides a powerful mechanism by which table and index data can be partitioned according to value ranges. Each partition can be stored in a different tablespace and each tablespace can then be placed on a different disk. Once a partition is set up it is very easy to alter or move partitions from one tablespace to another. DML operations can be applied to individual partitions and the cost-based optimizer can perform parallel operations against a partitioned table.

From a backup and recovery viewpoint partitions can be backed up and recovered individually whilst the remaining partitions are online and being accessed by users. If part of a table is lost, the DBA can restore the partition instead of the entire table making recovery much faster.

We will look at options for recovering partitions when we come to our backup/recovery examples in Chapter 8.

The new ROWID format

Oracle has also changed the format of the ROWID. The ROWID uniquely identifies a row in your database and is the fastest access path to the data. Due to the introduction of partitions, Oracle has had to introduce a new concept called the OBJECT ID and added it to the front of the ROWID. The format of the ROWID now looks like this:

Object ID	Relative File Number	Block Address	Slot Number
6 digits	3 digits	6 digits	3 digits

In Oracle7 the Relative File Number used to be unique to each database, in Oracle8 it is relative to the tablespace and it is the Object ID that spans the database.

Recovery Manager (RMAN)

Oracle's Recovery Manager (RMAN), first introduced with Oracle8, was briefly discussed in Chapter 2. We will be using various examples of how to use Recovery Manager for backup and recovery of SAP R/3 throughout the rest of the book.

4 Configuring SAP R/3 and Oracle

Part of a successful backup and recovery strategy involves correctly configuring both R/3 and Oracle. Correct configuration will make the backup and recovery process easier and less error prone.

4.1 SAP R/3 installation guidelines

4.1.1 Sizing the system

Why include a section on system sizing in a book about R/3 backup and recovery?

Well, the size of the database is vitally important when determining the amount of disk space required and, therefore, the number and type of disks needed to provide both the required transaction throughput, and database availability/reliability. The recovery of many R/3 systems is hampered by inadequate disk space and several database failures occur for this reason.

Sizing is a complex and, at best, inaccurate procedure. The goal of this process is to determine three vitally important figures:

- the amount of CPU power required (this determines the number of servers needed and the amount of memory each server needs to have);

- the total size of the database;

- the amount of network traffic.

The CPU requirements are usually based on the number of users per application module and the number of transactions each module is required to handle. SAP can provide loading factors for each of the R/3 modules that indicate the relative amount of CPU processing power each module needs.

Database sizing requires a more in-depth knowledge of the business and an intimate knowledge of the amount of data each module is capable of generating under different transaction loads. Often the initial estimates are far too low requiring additional disk capacity to be purchased after 'go-live'. Consequently the DBA may have to perform file system redesigns and time-consuming database reorganizations. File system redesigns will also involve changes to the backup and recovery procedures which can lead to errors being made and therefore potentially jeopardizing the backup/recovery process, putting the R/3 application at risk.

To avoid this situation it is wise to use a sizing tool that SAP makes available to their partners. This tool will calculate the amount of disk space required by the database for each R/3 application module being implemented. Information is fed into the sizing tool from business related questionnaires which are supplied by SAP and their partners. This tool will also calculate the estimated tablespace sizes and the largest tables they will include. It is important that the information fed into the tool is as accurate as possible to avoid file system reorganizations at a later date and the potential for lengthy downtimes of your R/3 system.

4.1.2   Database file system layout

The crucial factor for a successful SAP R/3 installation is distributing the data files across the available hard disks. This procedure requires a great deal of thought and planning, preferably before the installation of the R/3 system itself. The successful distribution of the database and non-database files is crucial to the performance, data security, database maintainability and reliability of your system. An inappropriate file system layout can impact the ease with which a DBA can perform routine data file maintenance and can severely limit the database backup and recovery options available.

The file systems can be classified as database independent and database dependent. The database independent file systems contain the SAP global data files and executables and are as follows:

- `/usr/sap/trans` – contains the global R/3 configuration file (`sapconf`) and is also used for the R/3 transport files.

- `/sapmnt/<SID>` – contains the system-wide data for a single R/3 system. Normally this directory is created on the central instance and its subdirectories are NFS mounted to the application servers.

- `/usr/sap/<SID>` – instance specific data with links to other directories.

Database dependent file systems are as follows:

- `/oracle/stage/stage_<VNUM>` – this directory is used for the installation and upgrade of Oracle (`<VNUM>` represents the Oracle version number).

- `/oracle/<SID>` – this is the top-level directory where the Oracle instance is installed. The Oracle instance name and the R/3 system name will be the same. There are several subdirectories under this top-level directory containing the database files for the R/3 tablespaces, a location for the online and archive redo logs, etc. These directories were explained in the previous chapter.

When determining how to distribute the data files across multiple disks and disk controllers the following factors need to be taken into account:

- **Data file size** – this is a very important parameter to determine as we discussed earlier. Making the file sizes too small will cause early maintenance problems leading to the need to add more data files and possibly affecting performance. Any data file changes will impact your backup and recovery plan.

- **Data integrity and security** – needs to be a major determining factor when deciding the location of various data files. You need to consider what type of recoveries you may need to perform on your R/3 system and therefore what type of backups you will perform and therefore where to place various data files. You will also need to consider what type of disk storage you have available. For example, if you are installing R/3 on RAID devices your data file placement strategy will differ from the strategy you would use if you were installing on non-RAID devices. We discuss this in more detail later in this section.

- **Performance** – also affects data file placement. Balancing input/output activity across multiple physical disks is one of the tasks facing a DBA. Some trade-off will have to be made between data file placement to obtain good performance and placement to achieve an acceptable level of data integrity and security. Once again, if using RAID devices your data file placement strategy has to change.

- **Growth** – needs to be considered also. Underestimating data volumes is a common mistake. Any decisions based on estimated volumes have to be questioned closely. Your strategy must include allowances for expanding the number of data files and the addition of more physical disks. You also need to consider what impact these changes will have on the maintenance of your backup and recovery procedures.

To help you determine how to map your data files to physical disks we will discuss some simple rules. We will first consider how these rules can help us to place data files on standard disks and then we will discuss how these rules have to be changed when configuring your database files on RAID devices.

Whilst planning the disk mapping it is important to consider the following points:

- **The database must be recoverable** – under no circumstances must your tablespace/disk mapping compromise your ability to recover any portion of your database. You would be amazed at the number of sites that forget this basic rule and always have to recover their entire database every time they have a problem.

- **Online redo logs must be mirrored** – make sure you dedicate a disk or two solely for your archive redo logs.

- **Avoid contention between Oracle background processes** – contention between the Oracle background processes DBWR, LGWR and ARCH will really constrain performance. Contention between these processes must be avoided at all costs.

- **Avoid contention between disks for DBWR** – the DBWR process must be able to perform I/Os to disk as soon as it needs to without having to wait for disks to become available.

These rules may seem to be very restrictive but if adhered to will ensure you achieve the maximum performance throughput from your database without compromising data integrity.

The optimal configuration for R/3 is to have every file system on a dedicated disk – this would mean that a typical R/3 installation would have 16 disks (excluding the operating system disks) of which most, if not all, would be mirrored making a total of 32 disks in all. Whilst this appears to be a simple and elegant solution, it can be wasteful of disk space as not all of the file systems require the same amount of disk space. To make better use of the disks some compromises have to be considered whilst still adhering as closely as possible to the above rules.

One compromise would be to combine the redo log directories in such a way that `/oracle/<SID>/origlogA` and `/oracle/<SID>/mirrorlogB` occupy the same disk and `/oracle/<SID>/origlogB` and `/oracle/<SID>/mirrorlogA` occupy another disk. Oracle would be writing synchronously to both sets of disks at the same time. Another compromise would be to place the `/oracle/<SID>/` and `/sapmnt/<SID>/` file systems on the same disk as they are not particularly high in I/O activity.

Whilst these rules and guidelines are relevant for standard disk configurations, they do not apply when installing your R/3 database on RAID devices. All of the good practices discussed in many books on Oracle configuration and tuning have to be changed if you wish to achieve both good performance and guaranteed data availability with RAID. There are currently seven RAID levels, numbered 0–6, which provide increasing levels of data protection from basic mirroring to full parity protection and 'hot-swappable' disk capabilities. Many organizations are implementing their R/3 Oracle databases on RAID-5 devices, which provide a high level of data protection and fault tolerance using parity data, others are avoiding RAID altogether because of performance problems. Again, when configuring RAID devices there has to be a trade-off between performance and data integrity. It is possible to provide both by utilizing RAID according to a new set of disk mapping rules, which we will discuss here.

Very often the DBA does not have a choice as to the type of disk devices that will be used with R/3 Oracle databases. The systems department, who are traditionally responsible for the purchase and supply of disk devices, will normally go for the maximum data availability option due to the critical nature of the R/3 application to the business. This means that RAID-5 disks are usually selected. The problem with RAID-5 is that it provides excellent data protection capabilities but at the expense of performance. Many companies have moved away from RAID-5 for this reason, and also because it can be expensive.

The first step in deciding which RAID level to use is to decide your main data file-mapping objective. Are you interested in optimizing data file placement for maximum performance, or maximum data protection? Very often the answer to this question is both! The good news for the DBA is that it is possible to find a compromise that can provide an acceptable solution for both apparently conflicting requirements. The first point to make is that some use of mirroring is essential for your R/3 application. This, combined with a sound backup and recovery strategy, is necessary to provide a 24hr x 7-day operation.

It must be understood that RAID devices will automatically provide I/O balancing across disks (it is actually the RAID disk controllers that do this). RAID is good for optimizing random I/Os but very often sequential I/O is slowed down. This affects the performance when writing and reading online and archived redo logs. It should be remembered that it is still possible to experience disk I/O bottlenecks with RAID devices, especially if traditional data file placement techniques are used.

The other feature provided by the RAID disk controller is read and write caching. From a backup and recovery viewpoint, write caching can be dangerous when used with a database. There is potential for data loss and no mechanism for recovering this data. When Oracle 'writes' to the RAID device the disk controller CPU logically writes the data to the write cache and indicates to Oracle that the write has taken place. If this write has been performed as part of a *commit* Oracle will destroy any rollback data because it assumes the write has been made permanent to disk. This will only occur when the write cache on the controller is full. This cache is usually battery-backed so should the power to the RAID cabinet fail the data should be protected and written to disk successfully. However should a power surge occur corrupting the data in the cache, or the battery unexpectedly fail, the data may be lost and not written to disk at all. It must be stressed that this possibility is remote but you must be aware of this possibility and accommodate it accordingly in your backup/recovery procedures.

When it comes to determining data file placement on RAID devices forget everything you have read in Oracle tuning and administration books. Instead separate your data files according to sequential and random I/O. Sequential I/O comes from the creation of indexes in the database, the Oracle LGWR background process when writing to and reading from the online and archive redo logs, Oracle's Import/Export utility and Oracle's SQL*Loader utility. Files associated with these processes should be placed on a separate logical volume (and disk controller) in your RAID cabinet. The remainder of your files fall into the random I/O category and should be placed on their own logical volume. Do not worry about the actual mapping of data files to physical disks in your RAID cabinet. Leave it to the disk controller(s) to do this for you. They will stripe your data either by block or stripe size depending on the level of RAID you are using. What you should do, however, is make sure you place the tablespaces containing the R/3 tables on the *same logical volume* as their associated indexes. For example, you should place the R/3 tablespace PSAPBTABD on the same logical volume as PSAPBTABI. But you should not place any

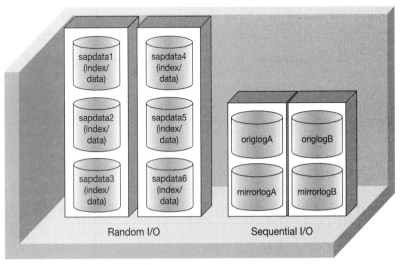

RAID cabinets

Figure 4.1   RAID configuration

other tablespaces on the same volume. So the general rule of thumb here is to place each data tablespace with its associated index tablespace on the same volume but only place one pair of tablespaces on each volume. Figure 4.1 shows an example configuration.

4.1.3   Centralized vs distributed R/3

The type of R/3 installation you are responsible for will determine your backup and recovery strategy. The backup needs of a centralized R/3 system differ slightly from those of a distributed one.

Due to the flexibility of R/3 it is possible to configure the system to run in a one-, two- or three-tier client/server architecture. The most common configuration is a central instance consisting of an application server (running the dialog, update, background, spool and enqueue services), a message server, a gateway and the database system. This typical configuration can be seen in Figure 4.2.

Another common configuration is one based on the three-tier client/server architecture where two or more application servers share the running of the various work processes, which in turn communicate with the database server. This configuration is illustrated in Figure 4.3. This distributed R/3 architecture provides higher system availability but at the same time demands a more complex backup and recovery strategy. The centralized instance is less complex but also less resilient in the case of failure.

The recommendations made in this book apply equally well to any R/3 configuration because our main topic is backup and recovery of the database that R/3 is accessing. In this case no matter what configuration you manage, the database server will generally be running on a single machine.

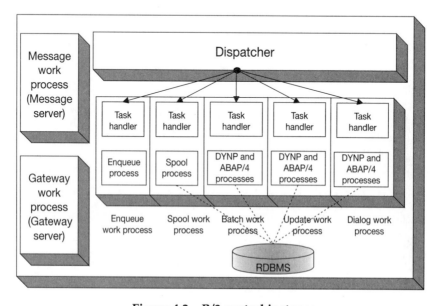

Figure 4.2   R/3 central instance

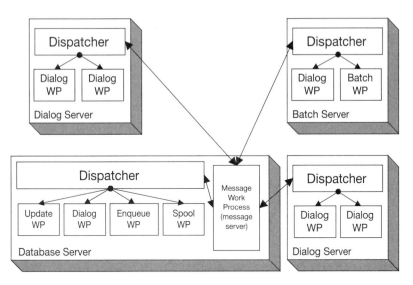

Figure 4.3   R/3 distributed architecture

4.1.4   Oracle Parallel Server

One of the so-called advantages of using the Oracle Parallel Server (OPS) configuration is the ability to be able to add additional machines to increase transaction throughput. This would appear to be attractive, particularly for those organizations that are experiencing a continually increasing workload. However, on closer inspection, R/3 is an OLTP (Online Transaction Processing) environment and simply adding extra nodes in such an environment does not automatically improve performance or transaction throughput. To understand why, it is important to know how OPS works.

Figure 4.4 shows the OPS architecture, consisting of multiple nodes accessing a single physical database. Each node runs a separate instance of Oracle and works independently of the other. When data needs to be shared across instances, the Oracle Parallel Cache Management and Distributed Lock Manager processes handle this.

Due to the fact that R/3 shares a large amount of data, installing R/3 in this environment has to be carefully planned. When multiple nodes require access to the same data, Oracle has to allocate the appropriate locks to ensure that any updates made to the data do not get overwritten. Oracle initially stores updates in the data buffers in the SGA of the instance where the update has taken place. Before other instances can see this data it has to be written to disk and then the next instance that needs to see this data has to be told it is on disk and ready to be read. Oracle performs this notification by 'pinging' the node on which the instance resides. Figure 4.5 shows this process.

When a lot of nodes require access to the same data at the same time this will cause excessive pinging that will slow down the performance of the database and therefore transaction throughput will suffer. To avoid this it is important to partition the R/3 workload across the available nodes such that they are performing autonomous tasks that

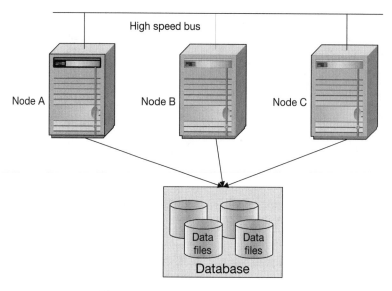

Figure 4.4   Oracle Parallel Server

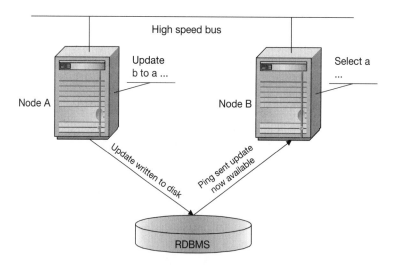

Figure 4.5   Example of pinging in an OPS environment

require a minimal amount of data sharing. One example would be in the R/3 logistics module, where several manufacturing plants will each access their own logistics data, unique to them, and will share a small amount of data with other plants. In this situation each plant could run on its own OPS node. Other types of partitioning could be based on application or task.

From a backup and recovery viewpoint, an OPS system behaves in a very similar way to a central, single-instance system. Each instance has its own SGA and background processes but it shares the raw data files and current control file which reside in a shared disk environment. Additionally, each instance has its own set of online and archived redo logs together with instance specific rollback segments. When backing up in this environment it is important to include the instance specific archived redo logs and rollback segments.

4.1.5   Oracle VLDB (Very Large Database)

SAP defines an Oracle VLDB as being a database that is larger than 20GB. Whilst this figure is subjective it is a useful guideline. If you are working with, or planning to work with, a database whose size is larger than this then you need to consider the issues discussed in this section very carefully. The discussion on data file mapping (see p. 32) is particularly relevant, as are our previous discussions on redo log and control file mirroring.

When looking at data file placement it is important to remember that the most intensive I/O will take place on the PSAPSTABD, PSAPCLUD and PSAPBTABD tablespaces together with their associated index tablespaces. Make sure these tablespaces are physically located on different disks (or different logical volumes if using RAID devices).

The sizes of your redo logs also become critical in VLDB environments. Remember you need to avoid frequent log switches so the redo log files must not be sized too small but also do not make them too large otherwise the redo logs will not be archived frequently enough. As mentioned earlier, by default R/3 creates logs that are 20MB in size. It would make sense to increase the log size to 50MB or even 100MB depending on the total size of your database.

You will also need to increase the size of the temporary tablespace PSAPTEMP to accommodate the larger data volumes that may be sorted and therefore require more temporary sort space. If your total database size exceeds 50GB then your temporary tablespace should be at least 1GB in size. You may also need to increase the size of your SYSTEM tablespace. You should consult the SAP OSS notes, which will give you the special procedures for increasing the sizes of these tablespaces.

You will need to consider adding more rollback segments to your PSAPROLL tablespace and therefore increasing the size of this tablespace. SAP recommends that each rollback segment must be able to handle the data generated by a maximum of four work processes. If you plan to have more than 40 work processes then you must create additional rollback segments to avoid redo data being overwritten.

Finally, you may also need to separate the larger tables from their actual tablespaces and to put them into their own tablespaces – SAP calls this procedure *table-stripping*. This procedure is performed from the SAPDBA program. Please see the R/3 documentation for details.

5

SAP R/3 backup guide

So far we have looked at the architecture of SAP R/3 and Oracle, looked at the critical components of the Oracle database to be considered for backup and recovery, and also briefly discussed the backup and recovery tools available. We will now turn our attention to how we backup both R/3 and Oracle.

5.1 An SAP R/3 backup strategy

5.1.1 Determining the correct backup strategy for your site

During the technical implementation of SAP R/3, it is essential to define the backup and recovery strategy that is to be used. When determining the backup strategy most appropriate for your needs you must bear in mind that the purpose of backups is to:

- avoid the loss of critical data due to a software or hardware failure;

- protect the business from excessive downtime of the R/3 system; and

- provide the ability to easily recover from a logical integrity error.

Your decisions are going to be determined by the following important points:

- **System availability**. The question you must answer first of all is how much downtime of the R/3 system is acceptable to the business. By determining this you will know the total length of time you have available for your backups to successfully complete before the system needs to be available again to the users. The size of this 'window' will determine exactly what is backed up and when. The system availability can range from 24x7 (24hrs per day x 7 days per week) which allows for no downtime, to maybe 15x5 which allows time at weekends and evenings for backups. Most companies have either moved to 24x7 availability of the R/3 system or are in the process of moving to this model. This requires that all backups be performed online whilst the database is being accessed.

- **What to back up**. Once you have determined the amount of available time you can dedicate to backups, you can then determine exactly what will be backed up and how often. This will involve determining how often you perform a full database backup, and whether you will include operating system files, R/3 runtime files, and other files such as the R/3 logs and the Oracle archived redo logs.

- **File sizes** The size of your data files will affect the total time it takes to backup. Therefore you need to consider how these files are to be backed up given that they will inevitably grow. The number of changes taking place to the data in your database will also affect the amount of Oracle redo data that is generated.

- **Type of backup**. You will need to determine what type of backup to perform. This will include the frequency with which you will perform a physical backup compared with a logical one, whether to perform full or incremental backups, and whether you need to verify the backup to ensure you can recover from it if necessary.

- **How the backup is to be performed**. It is important to decide how you are going to perform the backup by determining which tools you will use. You also need to consider where to run the backup. Will it be run on the machine where the database is located or on a separate machine in a client/server environment? This decision will be determined by the amount of available CPU power and network bandwidth you have at your disposal.

- **When to backup**. Critical to the R/3 backup strategy is a full database backup which must be taken regularly, and a frequent backup of the critical tablespaces such as PSAPBTABD, PSAPSTABD and PSAPCLUD. Other files can be backed up less frequently. It is normal for an R/3 backup strategy to contain different backup periods for different types of files. This decision will be determined by the system availability requirements, the expected time it will take to perform the backup, and the size of your database files.

- **Backup devices**. The hardware vendors now provide a startling array of backup devices, from simple tape systems to fully automated robotic devices that allow writing to tapes in parallel. The volume of data you are backing up, the speed with which you wish to write the backups, and the estimated growth of your data will determine the type of device you use.

- **Tape management**. The backup strategy must also define how tapes and/or other backup media are managed. This involves determining how they are labeled, their retention period, how often the tapes are recycled and where to store them.

- **Recovery procedures**. It is not unusual for an organization to define a clear set of backup procedures only to fail to decide and document the recovery procedures. It is only whilst trying to restore from backups that many problems can be found. Oracle Worldwide Customer Support have stated that over 36% of database recoveries fail because of inadequate or incorrect recovery procedures having been applied to the database by the DBA. This shows that many DBAs are unclear about what type of recovery needs to be performed when a database fails and a smaller percentage are unclear about how to recover at all. This book should be able to help with both situations. When documenting recovery procedures it is important to define all the possible failures that can occur on an R/3 system and to determine the recovery mechanism to use for each of these cases. For a discussion on the types of failures that can occur and how to recover from them please read Chapter 6 – SAP R/3 recovery guide. Chapter 8 discusses real life failures and how they were resolved.

- **Testing backup and recovery procedures**. Perhaps the most important step to take is to test both the backup and recovery procedures before they are put into production. This will ensure that the procedures being proposed actually work and achieve the aims of maintaining R/3 system availability and preventing data loss.

5.1.2   SAP backup recommendations

SAP makes the following recommendations to reduce the risks associated with backing up and recovering your database. These recommendations apply irrespective of the chosen backup strategy and backup tool(s) you use.

SAP's recommendations are:

- make sure that the Oracle ARCHIVELOG mode is switched on (see Chapter 3 for details on how to do this);

- make sure the control files are mirrored on different disks and disk controllers;

- mirror the online redo logs using either hardware mirroring, such as RAID-1 devices provide, or by using the Oracle redo log mirroring utilized by creating several redo log groups, or by using the redo log duplexing capability in Oracle8;

- separate the online and archived redo logs onto different disk devices;

- make sure that the Oracle and operating system block size are the same, 8K;

- make sure you understand the R/3 tablespace structure and monitor the tablespaces with the most activity. These are usually the PSAPBTABD, PSAPSTABD, PSAPCLUD, PSAPBTABI, PSAPSTABI, PSAPCLUI tablespaces;

- perform a full offline database backup weekly. This may not be possible if your R/3 system operates 24x7;

- perform a full online database backup daily;

- backup archived redo logs daily;

- perform a logical backup of the most critical tables daily.

SAP are in the process of making incremental backup strategies available, but at the time of publication they have not made any recommendations as to how these should be incorporated into the overall backup procedures.

5.1.3   Backup types

Physical vs logical

There are two types of backup that you will perform regularly on your R/3 database. A *physical* backup involves taking a copy of all of the relevant files including the database data files, control files, online redo logs, archived redo logs and any other R/3 specific files. This type of backup can be performed either by using an operating system utility, a third-party backup tool, or via the SAP supplied BRBACKUP and BRARCHIVE utilities.

A *logical* backup involves taking a copy of the database object structures (or more accurately, the SQL statements to create them) together with the SQL INSERT statements to recreate the data found in the R/3 tables at the time of the backup. A logical backup can be used to recover individual database objects and associated data rather than having to restore a complete backup. This type of backup cannot be performed with BRBACKUP, instead SAP recommends using Oracle Export. The author would suggest using a third-party tool for this due to the slow nature of the Oracle Export utility when executed against large databases.

You will notice from the SAP recommendations listed above, that you should perform an offline physical backup once a week together with an online physical backup every day. A logical backup should also be performed on a daily basis for all of the critical tables, i.e. those stored in the PSAPBTABD, PSAPSTABD and PSAPCLUD tablespaces.

5.2 How to backup SAP R/3

5.2.1 Using SAP supplied tools

BRBACKUP

SAP supplies three utilities for backing up and restoring your R/3 system. In this section we will discuss the BRBACKUP program; in the next section we will look at BRAR-CHIVE; and in Chapter 6 we will discuss BRRESTORE.

The backup program, BRBACKUP, can be run from the command line, or from within SAPDBA. The command line version is useful if you are using scripts to implement your backup procedures and you wish to run BRBACKUP directly from the scripts. Normally a DBA, or operations person responsible for running the backups, will execute the program from SAPDBA and it is this procedure that we shall discuss here. If you wish to know how to run BRBACKUP from the command line, please refer to the SAP R/3 online documentation.

BRBACKUP is used to not only backup the database files, control files and online redo logs, but it can also backup non-database files like the R/3 directories and log files. Backups can be run using CCMS functions from where backups can be scheduled and the backup logs can be viewed. When executing BRBACKUP from the SAPDBA main menu select option *h – Backup database*.

There are several things you must know in order to use BRBACKUP successfully:

- BRBACKUP is controlled by a parameter file that contains configuration information. The file, located in the /oracle/<SID>/dbs directory, is called init<SID>.sap.

- You should initialize all tapes that you plan to use because BRBACKUP requires a tape label.

- Select the tape drive configuration you want to use. Tape drives that implement hardware compression provide better backup performance when used with BRBACKUP.

- If you decide to use software compression instead, you have to use one of the SAPDBA functions to calculate the compression rate before you can perform a backup.

Now that you understand these prerequisites for using the tool, let's look at how we perform a backup from within SAPDBA. Figure 5.1 shows the main database backup menu, which is displayed after selecting the backup database option from the SAPDBA main menu.

On the left you can see the options available and on the right their current values (where applicable). These values are supplied from the BRBACKUP configuration file. By default BRBACKUP will perform an offline backup to a local tape device without compression. If you want a different default then you have to edit the configuration file. It is possible to dynamically change these parameters from the backup database menu. Before performing your first backup you need to edit the configuration file to make sure the path to your tape device is correct and that the tape length is correctly specified.

Let's take a look at each menu option.

a – **Backup function**. Selecting this option will display another menu allowing you to select the type of function you wish to perform. You can select from:

- **Normal backup** – which is the default.

- **Initialize BRBACKUP tape** – select this option when you need to initialize a tape the first time it is used. From this option you will be given a submenu allowing you to determine whether you want to check the tape label before initialization or not. If you select *no* for this option, you will be allowed to overwrite existing R/3 tape

```
                        Backup database

                                     Current value
     a - Backup function             Normal backup
     b - Parameter file              initPLAT1.sap
     c - Confirm backup parameters   no
     d - Language                    English
     e - Backup device type          tape
     g - Objects for backup          all
     h - Enter password interactively no
     i - Query only                  no
     j - Backup volume(s)
     k - Compress                    no
     l - Verification after backup   no
     m - Backup type                 offline
     n - Level of parallel execution O

     s - Start BRBACKUP
     q - Return

     Please select →
```

Figure 5.1   SAPDBA backup menu

volumes (so use with care). If you select *yes* the tape label will be checked and will only be initialized if the locking period has expired. From the submenu you will also be able to specify the number of tapes you want initializing.

- **Show information in tape header** – when selected, this option will display the full tape header allowing you to identify the date, label and backup type already present on the tape.

- **Determine compression rates** – this is the option you select if you want to use software compression. It will calculate the compression rate that BRBACKUP should use based on the amount and type of data it finds. The program will take account of the value for option *g* – *Objects for backup* when determining the compression rate. Running this function can take as long as performing the backup itself and should be run once every month to ensure you are using the optimal compression rate for your data.

b – **Parameter file**. This option allows you to specify which parameter file BRBACKUP should use. You may want to have different configuration files for performing offline and online backups for example.

c – **Confirm backup parameters**. By default this option is set to *no*. When set to *yes*, the user will have to confirm each parameter setting before BRBACKUP will proceed.

d – **Language**. This determines the language that the backup messages will be displayed in. The setting is *English* by default.

e – **Backup device type**. This option displays a valid list of backup device types, the default being backup to a local tape device. The other options available are:

- **Disk** – which will allow backups direct to disk. If you have sufficient disk space it is good practice to backup your online redo logs to disk and then copy them to tape later. Should you experience any problems with a redo log this will enable you to perform a faster recovery because you will not have to wait for the log to be recovered from tape first.

- **Pipe** – will allow the backup to be written to remote tape devices. It will force BRBACKUP to use the commands found in the configuration file to write to these devices.

- **Tape_auto** – suppresses tape switching messages. Use this when writing to automatic tape loading and switching devices such as robotic tape units.

- **Pipe_auto** – is a combination of the previous two options. This will write to an automatic tape loading or switching device that is remote.

- **Util_file** and **Util_file_online** – these options define the third-party backup tool which is integrated with BRBACKUP via the BACKINT interface. Only certified backup tools should be used. This parameter would be used to define the tape management software, for example. It is also possible to specify any parameters needed by the third-party tool, which will be passed at runtime. These parameters are defined in a parameter file the name of which is specified by the *Backup utility parameter file* option.

g – **Objects for backup**. From the submenu the following options are available:

- **All** – is the default value that will cause the entire database to be backed up.

- **Sap_dir/ora_dir** – will cause the SAP and Oracle directories to be backed up but NOT the database files. You would use this option to backup the SAP and Oracle software when first installed and after each upgrade.

- **Tablespace name** – will backup an individual tablespace.

- **File_id** – selecting this option will allow one or more Oracle data files to be backed up.

- **Generic path** – allows a specific file to be backed up. The full pathname and filename must be specified. Just entering a directory path will cause the contents of the entire directory to be backed up.

- **Object list** – will allow one or more database objects to be backed up individually.

h – **Enter password interactively**. When set to *yes* the user will be prompted to enter the DBA password. The default value is *no*.

i – **Query only**. This option displays a submenu of the following options:

- **No** – is the default value, which means that a backup will be performed.

- **With tape check** – will not perform a backup, instead it will display which tape volumes are required and will check that they are already mounted.

- **Without tape check** – will only display which tape volumes are required in order to successfully complete the backup. No backup will be performed and the tapes will not be checked.

j – **Backup volume(s)**. You can optionally enter here the tape label(s) to be used for the backup. If not supplied, the next sequential volume as defined in the configuration file, and as recorded in the backup logs, will be used. If specifying more than one tape volume, separate the label names with commas.

k – **Compress**. This option has three possible values:

- **No** – the default value which will cause backups to be performed without any form of compression.

- **Yes** – which will use software compression. Be sure to select the *Backup function →* *Determine compression rates* option so that BRBACKUP knows the compression rate to use.

- **Hardware** – select this option if your tape device has built-in hardware compression capability.

l – **Verification after backup**. This will verify the backup and make sure it can be read. The default value is *no* because verification can add significantly to the overall backup time.

m – **Backup type**. This option allows you to specify whether you want to perform an *offline* backup (R/3 must be shutdown in this case and BRBACKUP will automatically stop the database); *online* whereby a backup will be performed whilst R/3 is running; *offline_force* which will cause the database to be shutdown without checking the status of R/3.

n – **Level of parallel execution**. Here you specify the number of backup processes to run in parallel. The default value of 0 (zero) indicates that the number of processes will be the same as the number of backup devices.

After all of these options have been specified you must ensure that the required tapes are mounted and then select option *s – Start BRBACKUP*. While the backup proceeds, various status messages will be displayed on the terminal together with the estimated time of completion. Two log files are also created, a file called `back<SID>.log` containing a summary of the backup and a detailed log file called `b<timestamp>.<ext>`. Both of these files can be found in the `/oracle/<SID>/sapbackup` directory.

BRARCHIVE

The BRARCHIVE utility is provided by SAP to perform backups of the Oracle archived redo logs. In order to have a consistent backup you must back up these logs. By having these logs available you can perform point-in-time or partial database recoveries. If there are any logs missing then you will only be able to recover up to the point immediately before the missing log – all subsequent logs will be useless. It is essential to have access to these logs when performing logical recoveries, such as restoring an inadvertently deleted database object.

As previously discussed, Oracle will automatically copy the full online redo logs into the archive directory `/oracle/<SID>/saparch`, as long as the database is running in `ARCHIVELOG` mode which it must be for R/3. It is important to ensure that this directory is monitored constantly to avoid it filling up and stopping the Oracle database. There is a CCMS alert which will be raised should this situation occur. It would be better of course to make sure that this alert does not fire!

Like BRBACKUP, BRARCHIVE can be run either from the command line, or from SAPDBA. We will discuss how it is used from within SAPDBA. For an explanation of how to use it from a command line, or from within operating system command scripts, please refer to the SAP online documentation.

The configuration parameters are stored in the same parameter file as used by BRBACKUP (`init<SID>.sap`) which must be set before you start the program. The tape devices must be initialized before being written to by BRARCHIVE; you may consider using smaller tape capacities depending on the size of your redo logs.

To run BRARCHIVE select option *i – Backup archive logs* from the SAPDBA main menu. The backup archive logs menu will then be displayed, see Figure 5.2.

```
                        Backup archive logs

                                        Current value
        a - Archive function            Save archive logs
        b - Parameter file              initPLAT1.sap
        c - Confirm archive parameters  no
        d - Language                    English
        e - Archive device type         tape
        g - Number of redo logs         10000
        h - Enter password interactively no
        i - Query only                  no
        j - Archive volume(s)
        k - Compress                    no
        l - Verification after backup   no
        m - Continue until end of tape  no

        s - Start BRARCHIVE
        q - Return

        Please select →
```

Figure 5.2   SAPDBA backup archive logs menu

You will notice that this menu is very similar to the backup database menu. On the left you have all of the options available and on the right the current parameter settings for each option.

Let's take a look at each option in turn.

a – Archive function. This option allows you to specify which archiving function you want to perform. You will find it necessary to perform several of these functions depending on where you are in your backup schedule. For this reason it is good practice to create more than one parameter file with different archive function settings. When selecting this option a submenu will appear giving the following options:

- **Save archive logs** – this will backup all archive logs from the saparch directory that have not yet been saved. This is the default setting.

- **Make second copy of archive logs** – performs a second backup of the archived redo logs already backed up. You would use this option if you wanted to take another copy, for security purposes, to a different set of tapes but only had a single tape device available.

- **Double save archive logs (parallel)** – this copies the archive logs to two separate tape devices in parallel. This avoids the need to perform the first option followed by the second one providing you have more than one tape device.

- **Save and delete archive logs** – this will back up the archive logs and delete them from the `saparch` directory, once they have been successfully saved. If, for some reason, an archived log is not saved successfully it will not be deleted. By deleting the saved archived logs you are freeing up space in the saparch directory, thereby minimizing the risk of the directory filling up and stopping the database.

- **Make second copy and delete archive logs** – makes a second copy and then deletes the saved archive logs.

- **Double save and delete archive logs** – saves the logs to two tape devices in parallel and then deletes the saved logs.

- **Delete saved archive logs** – deletes all the archived logs that were previously backed up.

- **Make second copy and save archive logs** – this option is slightly different in that it makes a second copy of the archive logs that have already been saved and then will backup any new logs created since the last save.

- **Make second copy, delete, and save archive logs** – performs the same action as the previous option but in addition deletes the saved archive logs.

- **Initialize BRARCHIVE tape** – this is the same as the BRBACKUP option described earlier. There is one option which is different, **Stop BRARCHIVE run with fill option**, which stops a currently executing archive log backup that was started with the option **Continue until end of tape.**

b – **Parameter file, c – Confirm archive parameters, d – Language**. These three options are the same as for BRBACKUP.

e – **Archive device type**. Selecting this option will display a list of device types supported by BRARCHIVE. This list is the same as for BRBACKUP with one exception. The **disk** option can only be used if you are using the Oracle Parallel Server option (OPS) with R/3.

g – **Number of redo logs**. This option is set to 10,000 by default. This is the total number of redo logs to be backed up in a single run. Under no circumstances should your system have anywhere near this number of redo logs (unless they are very small indeed). By changing this value you can define how many redo logs should be backed up, BRARCHIVE will then backup the specified number of logs. For example if you have 10 archived redo logs available for backup and you set this parameter to 5, BRARCHIVE will backup the 5 oldest archive redo logs. It is advisable to leave this option to the default to ensure you always backup all of your logs.

h – **Enter password interactively, i – Query only**. These options are the same as for BRBACKUP.

j – **Archive volume(s)**. This option is the same as for the BRBACKUP utility. One point you must remember though is that if BRARCHIVE is unable to fit an archive redo log onto a single tape then you must restart BRARCHIVE to backup the remaining log files.

k – **Compress, l** – **Verification after backup**. Same as for BRBACKUP.

m – **Continue until end of tape**. The default value for this parameter is *no*. This causes BRARCHIVE to backup the archive redo logs according to the archive function chosen. When set to *yes* BRARCHIVE will backup new archive redo logs as they are generated. The process will stop when the tape is full or when stopped by selecting the **Stop BRARCHIVE run with fill option**.

After all of these options have been specified you must ensure that the required tapes are mounted and then select option *s* – *Start BRARCHIVE*. While the backup proceeds, various status messages will be displayed on the terminal together with the estimated time of completion.

5.2.2   Using Oracle supplied tools

Oracle7 backups

Most SAP R/3 sites use either the SAP supplied utilities for backing up their database, or some third-party SAP certified backup tool, which uses the BACKINT interface to R/3. A third approach is to use the tools supplied with the database by Oracle Corporation. We shall discuss in this section how to backup an Oracle7 database, and in the next section we shall look at Oracle8. It must be pointed out that any backups of your R/3 database performed with the Oracle utilities will not be recorded in the R/3 backup logs. It is the DBA's responsibility to ensure that any backup scripts that are used write the progress of the backups to a log file. This will assist with debugging any problems that may occur during the backup.

With Oracle7 it is possible to perform both logical and physical backups of the database; these backups can be taken both online and offline. Physical backups are normally performed using a UNIX operating system backup utility such as `tar` or `cpio`. When performing offline backups the R/3 system must be stopped and the Oracle database shutdown. For online backups both R/3 and Oracle will remain online but certain commands need to be executed before the database files are backed up. Logical backups are performed using the Oracle `Export`/`Import` utility. The author would recommend you stop R/3 before performing backups with this utility. You should also consider using a third-party tool for your logical backups as Oracle Export can be very slow when backing up large tables.

Physical backups

To perform a cold physical backup of your R/3 database you must first stop R/3 and then shutdown Oracle. R/3 and Oracle can be stopped by logging on to the server where R/3 and Oracle are running and executing the command `stopsap ALL`. This command will first stop all R/3 processes running on the machine followed by the Oracle database. You must log in as the R/3 system administrator to execute this command – the administrator account is normally *<SID>adm*. It is also possible to stop R/3 from CCMS but it is not currently possible to stop the database this way. To check that all of the R/3 processes have stopped run the following UNIX command `ps -eaf | grep dw`. Depending on the UNIX operating system you are using the command options may differ slightly.

If you are running distributed R/3 then you must execute the `stopsap` command on each application server before stopping the Oracle database. In this case you will use the command `stopsap R3` on all servers where only R/3 processes are running followed by the `stopsap ALL` command on the database server itself. It is possible to write a script to perform the shutdown of all application servers remotely using the remote shell function in UNIX. Be aware that the use of a remote shell may contravene your site security procedures, so check first!

The following files should be backed up when performing a weekly cold database backup:

- all database data files

- all control files

- all online redo logs

- all archived redo logs

- optionally, the `init<SID>.ora` file.

To backup all of these files it is necessary to use a UNIX operating system backup command such as `cpio` or `tar`. Which one you use is a matter of preference but you might like to bear in mind that BRBACKUP uses `cpio`. Most Oracle DBAs tend to prefer the `tar` command. The following example shows a sample UNIX `tar` command which is used here to backup the R/3 tablespace data files to a tape device called `/dev/rmt/0hc`

```
tar -cvf /dev/rmt/0hc /oracle/<SID>/sapdata[1-5]
```

You will need additional `tar` commands to backup the online redo log, archived redo log and control file directories.

Cold backups may only be performed when the database is shut down. In a 24x7 operation this is not possible so the alternative is to perform a daily hot backup of your database. A hot backup should be performed during periods of least user activity for two reasons. Firstly, the physical files are backed up using operating system commands that will consume most of the available CPU, thereby affecting online users. Second, a large amount of redo records will be generated by transactions that are executing during the period of the backup. Therefore the fewer transactions that can be performed against the database the better.

The following files should be backed up when performing a daily hot database backup:

- all data files

- all archived redo logs

- one control file.

The author recommends backing up one tablespace at a time according to the following backup procedure:

- Backup each tablespace:
  - put the tablespace into backup mode
  - backup all data files belonging to the tablespace
  - take the tablespace out of backup mode.
- Backup the archived redo logs:
  - temporarily stop the Oracle archiving background process
  - determine which files are in the archive redo log directory
  - restart the Oracle archiving background process
  - backup the archived redo logs and then make a second copy of them to a backup destination on disk and delete them from the archive redo log directory, or, if insufficient disk space, just delete them.
- Backup the control file using the Oracle command ALTER DATABASE BACKUP CONTROLFILE.

When backing up the tablespace data files it is preferable to back them up to disk first, then copy them to tape later. This will speed up the backup process significantly.

Performing a logical backup

In addition to the physical backups, SAP recommend you take a logical backup of your most critical tables. It is then possible to restore these tables individually should you experience problems with them later. Oracle provides the Export/Import utilities for this purpose. Export performs a logical backup whilst Import performs a restore from a logical backup.

Export reads the database and Oracle data dictionary and writes its output to a binary file containing all of the SQL commands needed to recreate the backed up objects and data. It is possible to backup individual tables, all objects owned by a particular user, or the entire database. You also have the option to backup the grants, user roles, indexes and constraints of the tables you are backing up. Export will allow you to perform incremental backups which can be one of two types: *cumulative*, which backs up all objects that have changed since the last full database export, or *incremental*, which backs up all objects that have changed since the last export.

SAP recommends only performing logical backups of your most critical tables, i.e. those tables found in the PSAPBTABD, PSAPSTABD and PSAPCLUD tablespaces. You may also consider objects in other tablespaces to be critical to your system so you should include these too. To implement this requirement using Oracle's Export you should select the *table mode*, which will export the tables you specify together with the indexes and other data dictionary objects.

Export is run from the command line and the required parameters can either be entered interactively, or from a command file. The latter approach is recommended so that the export can be executed directly from a shell script without user intervention.

Export uses the following parameters:

- **USERID** – the username/password of the account running the export. This should be the R/3 user that owns the database objects.

- **BUFFER** – the size of the data buffer used to fetch the rows. This should be set to a value greater than 64000 bytes.

- **FILE** – the name of the output file that will contain the logical backup. This defaults to `expdat.dmp`.

- **COMPRESS** – this parameter determines whether the table being backed up should be compressed into a single extent. Export will store the storage clause with the table definition. If this parameter is set to the default of *yes* and subsequently you restore the table, the Import utility will store all of the table data in a single contiguous extent.

- **GRANTS** – this parameter determines whether the grants on this object will be saved. Defaults to *yes* and should not be changed.

- **INDEXES** – the setting of this parameter determines whether the indexes should be saved. Defaults to *yes* and should not be changed.

- **ROWS** – determines if the table data is to be exported. Defaults to *yes* and should not be changed.

- **CONSTRAINTS** – determines if the tables constraints are to be exported. Defaults to *yes* and should not be changed.

- **FULL** – if set to *yes* Export will perform a full database export. When performing the logical backup of your R/3 tables this parameter should be left to the default of *no*.

- **OWNER** – causes Export to backup all objects owned by the username defined for this parameter. This parameter should not be used when performing an R/3 logical backup unless you want to perform a logical backup of all R/3 objects.

- **TABLES** – a list of tables to be backed up. When export is run interactively these table names are entered individually. For your R/3 backups it is preferable to specify these in the parameter file.

- **RECORDLENGTH** – defines the length, in bytes, of each record in the output file. This parameter can safely be left to the default value.

- **INCTYPE** – this defines the type of backup being performed. The choices are:

  COMPLETE – which is the default value and backs up all the specified objects irrespective of whether they have changed since the last backup or not.

  CUMULATIVE – which will backup tables whose rows have changed since the last cumulative or complete export.

  INCREMENTAL – which will backup tables whose rows have changed since the last full export.

  The *CUMULATIVE* and *INCREMENTAL* exports can only be used if the setting of the **FULL** parameter is yes. This means that if you are performing a logical backup of only your most critical R/3 tables, as recommended by SAP, you can only perform a complete export each time. If you want to perform an incremental backup you must use either BRBACKUP or a third-party tool which allows incremental backups.

- **RECORD** – for INCREMENTAL backups this parameter determines whether the backup is recorded in the Oracle data dictionary tables. Defaults to *yes*.

- **PARFILE** – the name of the file containing the parameter values. The author recommends using this file to simplify the R/3 backup procedure.

- **ANALYZE** – this parameter indicates whether statistics about each exported object should be written to the output file. Defaults to ESTIMATE which will cause Oracle to estimate the statistics for the object rather than performing a full analysis.

- **CONSISTENT** – tells Export to backup read consistent versions of all the tables. This is needed if the data in the tables being exported is changing during the export. It is not recommended to perform a logical backup of your tables while R/3 is running. The default setting for this parameter is *no*.

- **LOG** – the name of the file to which logging information is to be written.

Once you have determined the correct settings for each of these parameters place them in a parameter file so that they can be used every time you run your daily logical backup. Please refer to the Oracle documentation for the format of the parameter file.

To execute the export you would use the command `exp parfile=r3logical.par`. This would normally be executed from within a shell script.

Oracle8 backups

With Oracle8 came a new tool designed, according to Oracle Corporation, to make backup and recovery easier. One of the major criticisms made about Oracle7 was the slow and cumbersome procedures required to backup the database; Oracle's answer was to produce Recovery Manager (RMAN). In this section we will look at how RMAN works and how to perform the different backup types required for R/3.

RMAN is a command line tool that will backup and restore the database to which it is connected. Backups can be performed to tape and can only be restored by RMAN. Alternatively the DBA can backup to disk and then has the option to either recover using RMAN or manually as with Oracle7. An Oracle server process is responsible for backing up and restoring data files, control files and archived redo logs. RMAN stores details about each backup and recovery in either an Oracle database, known as a catalog, or in the database control files. If control files are used it is not possible to perform a point-in-time recovery.

RMAN can be executed from Oracle Enterprise Manager (OEM) which provides a GUI interface and therefore the DBA can use point and click functionality to specify and execute backups. It is important to note that the Oracle7 backup, restore and recovery methods are still supported in Oracle8. It is also important to note that, from R/3 release 4.5A, SAP has integrated RMAN with SAPDBA. See the section headed RMAN and SAPDBA later in this chapter.

RMAN catalog

If you decide to use the RMAN catalog to store your backup and recovery information you must first create the catalog in an Oracle8 database. It is important to ensure that the catalog is created in a database that is separate from the one you are backing up. Should your database fail you will need access to the catalog before you can recover it.

To create the catalog you must perform the following steps:

1. Create a user that will be the owner of the catalog. Remember to create it in a separate database from your R/3 instance.

2. Grant `connect, resource` and `recovery_catalog_owner` privileges to the user created in step 1.

3. Create the catalog tables by running the `catrman.sql` script.

Figure 5.3 shows a catalog being created.

```
SVRMGR>   connect <username>/<password>
Connected.
SVRMGR>   create user rman identified by <password>
     2> default tablespace <tablespace name>
     3> temporary tablespace <tablespace name>;
Statement processed.
SVRMGR>   grant connect, resource to rman;
Statement processed.
SVRMGR>   grant recovery_catalog_owner to rman;
Statement processed.
SQL>   @<path name>catrman.sql
(Various messages displayed here ...)
SQL>   exit
```

Figure 5.3   Creating an RMAN catalog

The next step is to register the R/3 database in the catalog. This is performed by executing RMAN and at the command line running the `REGISTER DATABASE` command, after having connected to both the R/3 instance and the Oracle8 instance containing the catalog.

The catalog is updated automatically after any backup or restore operation, however information about the online and archived redo logs is *not* automatically updated. This must be performed manually by the DBA. The author recommends you re-synchronize the catalog every day using the RMAN `RESYNC CATALOG` command as shown in Figure 5.4.

```
RMAN> resync catalog;
RMAN-03022: compiling command: resync
RMAN-03023: executing command: resync
RMAN-08002: starting full resync of recovery catalog
RMAN-08004: full resync complete
```

Figure 5.4   Executing the RESYNC CATALOG command in RMAN

Performing backups with RMAN

Let us now look at how we perform database backups with RMAN.

RMAN supports all types of backups except *logical backups*, which still need to be performed using the Export utility. It is possible to perform backups of the entire database, individual tablespaces, data files, control files and archive redo logs. Oracle recommends that you **do not backup online redo logs**. The reason for this is that when faced with a failed R/3 database, the DBA may inadvertently recover a complete backup and overwrite the online redo logs potentially losing data that was not written to an archived redo log copy. For this reason online redo logs should not be backed up in Oracle8.

RMAN can perform full and incremental backups, together with image copies of data files. Operating system backups are also supported. Image copies do not require any recovery and can be used directly to replace the original file. Image copies are taken in RMAN using the COPY command that causes an Oracle process, not the operating system, to copy the data file. It is not necessary to place the tablespace in backup mode before performing such a copy.

Backup sets are created using the BACKUP command and can contain *either* data files *or* archive redo log files, not both. A full backup contains all blocks that are being used by the database. This should not be confused with a backup of the entire database which will include all data blocks contained within the database whether they are in use or not.

Incremental backups will cause RMAN to copy only the data blocks which have changed since the last backup and the DBA has the option of performing both cumulative and non-cumulative incremental backups.

Finally, operating system backups can also be performed and registered in the catalog. The tablespace would have to be placed in backup mode using the ALTER TABLESPACE <tablespace name> BEGIN BACKUP command, backed up using an operating system utility such as tar or cpio, and registered in the catalog using the CATALOG command in RMAN. Of course the ALTER TABLESPACE <tablespace name> END BACKUP command would need to be executed.

Physical backups

To perform a cold physical backup of your R/3 database with RMAN you must first stop R/3 and then shutdown Oracle. This is performed as described earlier for Oracle7 physical backups.

The following files should be backed up when performing a weekly cold database backup of R/3 with RMAN:

- all database data files

- all control files

- all archived redo logs

- optionally, the `init<SID>.ora` file.

You will need to create *two* backup data sets. The first data set will contain the data files and control files, whilst the second will contain the archived redo log files. Optionally you may decide to create a third data set by backing up the control files separately from the data files. It is not necessary to do this.

It is important with R/3 to perform a *consistent backup* of the database. This ensures that the data files and control files are consistent to a point-in-time. If you need to restore from this backup it will not be necessary for Oracle to apply the redo logs and therefore recovery will be faster. It is possible to perform an *inconsistent backup* with RMAN but in this case redo logs would need to be applied when recovering.

Figure 5.5 shows how to perform a backup of your data files and control files whilst the database is open and running in `ARCHIVELOG` mode. Remember the R/3 instance must have been stopped prior to running this type of backup.

```
RMAN> run {
2> allocate channel c1 type 'tape';
3> backup full filesperset 3
4> (database format 'SAPR3FULL%t%s.%p');
5> }
```

Figure 5.5 Full database backup using RMAN

Figure 5.6 shows how to perform a backup of the archived redo logs. It is possible to backup individual archived logs based on timestamps or log sequence numbers but the author recommends using the `ALL` option to backup all archived redo logs daily.

```
RMAN> run {
2> allocate channel c1 type 'tape';
3> sql 'alter system archive log current';
4> backup archivelog all
5> format 'SAPR3LOGS%t%s.%p');
6> }
```

Figure 5.6 Backing up all archivelogs using RMAN

To backup the `init<SID>.ora` file it is necessary to backup using an operating system command. This operation cannot be recorded in the RMAN catalog.

Hot physical backup

As discussed earlier, SAP recommends a weekly cold physical backup together with a daily hot database backup. If you are running R/3 in a 24x7 operation then your only option is to perform daily hot physical backups to adequately secure your data.

Our discussion of Oracle7 hot database backups listed the files that must be backed up. They are:

- all data files

- all archived redo logs

- one control file.

Unlike Oracle7 hot backups, it is not necessary to backup each tablespace individually because RMAN is able to perform the backup without the DBA having to execute the `ALTER TABLESPACE <tablespace name> BEGIN/END BACKUP` commands. Instead RMAN takes a snapshot of all data file headers before starting the hot backup on the tablespace. At this point it has recorded the System Change Number (SCN) at the beginning of the backup. The advantage here is that no extra redo is generated whilst the tablespace is being backed up. This also gives the DBA the flexibility to perform either a whole database backup using the approach taken in Figure 5.5, or a tablespace level backup as shown in Figure 5.7 below. The only difference is that during these backups the R/3 system is open and available to users.

```
RMAN> run {
2> allocate channel c1 type disk;
3> backup tablespace 'psapbtabd'
4> filesperset 3
5> format 'PSAPBTABD%t%s.%p';
6> }
```

Figure 5.7   Backing up an individual tablespace using RMAN

When backing up the tablespace data files it is preferable to back them up to disk first, then copy them to tape later. This will speed up the backup process significantly.

Should you decide to perform a hot tablespace backup you must remember to either separately backup the database control file, or include the control file as part of the tablespace backup. You can create a backup set containing the control file through RMAN as shown in Figure 5.8. In Figure 5.9 we give an example of a tablespace backup which includes the control file in the same backup set.

```
RMAN> run {
2> allocate channel c1 type disk;
3> backup current controlfile
4> format 'SAPcntrl%t%s.%p';
5> }
```

Figure 5.8   Backing up the current control file using RMAN

```
RMAN> run {
2> allocate channel c1 type disk;
3> backup tablespace 'psapbtabd'
4> including current controlfile
5> format 'PSAPBTABD%t%s.%p';
6> }
```

Figure 5.9   Tablespace backup including control file using RMAN

It is also possible to create an image copy of a control file using the COPY command.
To backup the archived redo logs follow the procedure as shown in Figure 5.6.

Logical backups with RMAN

It is not possible to perform logical backups with RMAN, instead the Oracle Export utility
should be used. This was discussed in detail in the previous section headed **Performing a
logical backup**.

Incremental backups

If you are responsible for a very large R/3 database then you may not have a sufficiently
large batch window within which to perform full database or tablespace backups. The alternative is to perform an incremental backup so that you are only backing up the data blocks
that have changed since the last backup was run. One disadvantage is that recovery may
take longer, due to the fact that several incremental backups may need to be applied, but the
advantage is that less space will be required on your backup devices for each backup.

A logical incremental backup can be performed using the Export utility as described earlier. RMAN is able to perform physical incremental backups, which can be both *cumulative*
and *non-cumulative*. A *cumulative* backup contains all data block changes that have occurred
since the last backup at a lower level. This type of backup eases restoration due to the fact
that all block changes are held in the same backup set. A *non-cumulative* backup only
includes blocks that have changed since the previous backup at the same or lower level. In
this case more than one backup may be required to restore all of the required blocks.

When performing incremental backups with RMAN the DBA decides the backup level, which determines whether the backup is *cumulative* or *non-cumulative*. As an example we may decide to perform the following types of backup on the days given:

- Sunday – a full database backup at level 0.

- Monday and Tuesday – a non-cumulative incremental backup at level 2. This will backup all block changes made since the last backup at either level 2 or lower. In our example, Monday's backup would contain block changes made since Sunday, and Tuesday's backup would include block changes made since Monday. If we had a failure on Wednesday we would have to apply Sunday's backup followed by both Monday's and Tuesday's.

- Wednesday – a non-cumulative backup at level 1. This backup will include all data block changes made at the same or lower level. Because we have specified the level as 1, this means that all block changes made since Sunday's backup will be recorded in the backup set. In effect we have now consolidated Monday, Tuesday and Wednesday's backups into one backup set. Should we now get a failure we only need to restore the backup from Sunday and Wednesday.

- Thursday, Friday and Saturday – a non-cumulative backup at level 2. This will record block changes made since the previous day's backup.

- Sunday – a full database backup at level 0.

For further information on incremental backups please refer to Chapter 7 of the *Oracle8 Server Backup and Recovery Guide*.

Using scripts with RMAN

The backup examples we have used assume you are inputting the relevant RMAN commands directly from the command line. In order to avoid unnecessary errors, and to make the backup procedures more automated, it is recommended that you write and use backup scripts when executing such commands. RMAN has the ability to use scripts that are stored in its catalog, or that are available on disk. By storing the scripts in the catalog you can use RMAN to maintain them.

To create a script simply use either the CREATE SCRIPT or REPLACE SCRIPT command. Figure 5.10 shows a script being created using the CREATE SCRIPT command.

```
RMAN> create script SAPR3_full {
1> allocate channel c1 type 'tape';
2> backup full filesperset 3
3> (database format 'SAPR3FULL%t%s.%p');
4> }
```

Figure 5.10   Creating and storing a script in the RMAN catalog

To execute a stored script use the EXECUTE SCRIPT command as shown in Figure 5.11.

```
RMAN> run {
2> execute script SAPR3_full;
3> }
```

Figure 5.11   Executing a stored script

There is also a DELETE SCRIPT command, which removes a previously stored script from the catalog. At the time of writing, this command had not been implemented.

The output from RMAN can be captured to a log file, which is highly recommended. This is achieved by using the msglog parameter on the command line.

RMAN and SAPDBA

From R/3 release 4.5A, SAP has integrated the functionality of RMAN within SAPDBA. This means that when any backup functions are performed from the SAPDBA menus, RMAN will be invoked to perform the requested function. The advantages of this integration are as follows:

- The RMAN catalog is not used. SAPDBA forces RMAN to write the backup information to the current control file and backs up this file after every backup. During a recovery the control file is restored first, then the relevant data files.

- Because RMAN is being run from within SAPDBA, backups can be monitored from within CCMS and the usual backup logs are written.

- All previous backup strategies can still be used with RMAN.

- Incremental backups can be performed, as described earlier. Only level 0 (full database) and cumulative level 1 incremental backups are supported.

- Normally RMAN only backs up database files. The integration ensures your non-database files, such as R/3 logs, are backed up as well if required.

- Both BRBACKUP and BRRESTORE can verify RMAN backups.

You should be aware that RMAN has no relevance when performing offline redo log backups with BRARCHIVE, when backing up standby databases, or split mirror backups. For further details please refer to the SAP online documentation on SAPnet (*http://sapnet.sap-ag.de*).

Tape management

As part of your R/3 backup strategy you must define your approach to tape management. You should decide how you are going to physically label your tapes, the retention period of each backup according to the backup type, how many tape copies you will keep and how many will be sent offsite for disaster recovery purposes.

Depending on the backup software you use different tape management facilities are available. The BRBACKUP utility supplied by SAP will allow you to specify, for example, the retention period of your backup tapes. The program uses this parameter to determine if a tape volume can be overwritten. Oracle's RMAN can interface with third party tape management software products that provide comprehensive tape and robotic device support. One such product, Legato Networker Lite, is supplied with Oracle8. Third-party vendors also provide support for tape management products from their backup tools.

Split mirror backup

A split mirror backup allows you to perform a backup from the mirrored copy of your database. This approach to backing up your R/3 system has several advantages:

- It allows you to perform an *offline backup* of the database with only minimal downtime of your production system.

- An *online backup* can be executed from a backup machine avoiding any performance hit on your production system during the backup. This involves running BRBACKUP on a machine that is separate from your production system.

- Both types of backup can be monitored within CCMS from your production system.

- The BACKINT interface for third-party tools supports a split mirror backup, so any certified products using this interface can also be used to perform this type of backup on your system.

Online split mirror backups are only available with SAP R/3 release 4.x. Figure 5.12 shows the architecture of the split mirror backup.

In order to be able to perform a split mirror backup, the following conditions must be met:

- For SAP R/3 release 3.1, the full Oracle database software (version 7.3 and above) must be installed on the backup machine. For release 4.0 upwards, only the Oracle client software is required, which can be any version of Oracle supported by SAP.

- The Oracle directory structure should be identical to the R/3 installation on your production machine.

- The `/oracle/<SID>/sapbackup` directory should be mounted from the backup machine on the primary machine.

- The profile for BRBACKUP should be available on the backup machine.

- The R/3 profile, `init<SID>.sap`, must have the parameter `backup_type` set to one of the following:

  — for release 3.1 `backup_type = offline_standby`

  — for release 4.0 `backup_type = offline_split`, when performing an *offline backup*, or `backup_type = online_split`, when performing an *online backup*.

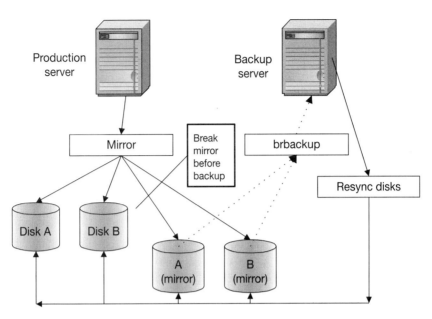

Figure 5.12   SAP R/3 split mirror architecture

- There must be a SQL*Net connect string defined so that there is communication available between the backup and production machines. Please refer to the SAP document *Split Mirror Disk Backup*, available on SAPnet (*http://sapnet.sap-ag.de*), for details on how to do this.

- The backup machine must have the executables installed for BRBACKUP, BRCONNECT and BRTOOLS.

- If you are using a third-party backup tool in a split mirror configuration, this product may have additional installation requirements. You should refer to the documentation for your chosen product.

- In order to split the mirror before backing up (see the backup procedure described later in this section), it will be necessary to execute a command that performs the split. This command is specific to the type of mirrored disks you are using and you should refer to the disk manufacturer's documentation for details. This command should be defined in the init<SID>.sap profile using the parameter split_cmd = <manufacturer specific split command>.

- After the backup has taken place, the mirror will have to be resynchronized. This is performed using a manufacturer specific resync command. This command should be defined using the resync_cmd parameter in the init<SID>.sap profile.

Subject to the above conditions being met, you can now perform a split mirror backup. If you are running SAP R/3 release 3.1 then you can only perform an *offline backup* using a split mirror. This means that the production database will be down for a short time to bring the database to a consistent state. The database will be available again once the backup starts. During this time it is not necessary to shutdown the R/3 system, as the processes will automatically reconnect to the database.

Split mirror offline backup

In an *offline backup* the database is brought down whilst the mirror disks are split. The mirror is then resynchronized on successful completion of the backup. In the following procedure, if you are running SAP R/3 release 4.0, steps 1, 2, 3 and 5 are performed automatically by BRBACKUP. If you are running release 3.1, you must perform these steps manually.

To perform an *offline backup* the procedure is as follows:

- If running release 4.0, start BRBACKUP on the backup machine (backup_type = offline_split).

- Shut down the database on the production machine to bring the database to a consistent state for backup. Do not worry about shutting down the R/3 system, the work processes will reconnect to the database automatically when it is reopened. This will be performed automatically by BRBACKUP in SAP R/3 release 4.0.

- Split the mirror disks using the command defined for the split_cmd parameter in the profile init<SID>.sap. This will be performed automatically by BRBACKUP in SAP R/3 release 4.0.

- Restart the production database. This will be performed automatically by BRBACKUP in SAP R/3 release 4.0.

- Perform the offline backup of the mirror disks using BRBACKUP. If using SAP R/3 release 3.1 you will start BRBACKUP on the backup machine for the first time at this point.

- On successful completion of the backup, synchronize the mirror disks with the production disks using the command defined for the resync_cmd parameter in the profile init<SID>.sap. This will be performed automatically by BRBACKUP in SAP R/3 release 4.0. Depending on the manufacturer, for example EMC, the resync process may not consume any CPU on the backup or production machine because the CPU on the disk controller will perform it.

Split mirror online backup

An *online backup* in a split mirror environment can be performed with SAP R/3 release 4.0 upwards. To perform an *online backup* the procedure is as follows (all of these steps will be performed automatically by BRBACKUP):

- Start BRBACKUP on the backup machine.

- Set the tablespaces to be saved to backup status using the ALTER TABLESPACE BEGIN BACKUP command.

- Split the mirror disks using the command defined for the `split_cmd` parameter in the profile `init<SID>.sap`.

- Reset the tablespaces to their normal state using the ALTER TABLESPACE END BACKUP command. This stops the generation of additional redo log data by Oracle which would normally be generated during the whole of the backup process.

- Backup the mirror disks.

- On successful completion of the backup, synchronize the mirror disks with the production disks using the command defined for the `resync_cmd` parameter in the profile `init<SID>.sap`.

6 SAP R/3 recovery guide

During operation of the R/3 system different types of software problems and hardware failures may arise causing inconsistencies in the integrity of the R/3 data. This gives rise to the need to restore data from a backup. The number and types of problems that can lead to data corruption and/or loss of data are significant. This chapter looks at the significant types of failures that you may experience during day-to-day running of SAP R/3 and how to recover from them. Chapter 8 also discusses some real-life problems that have occurred on SAP R/3 sites around the world and shows how those problems were resolved.

Restore and recovery procedures should be practiced frequently. By doing so, the DBA can assess whether the backup strategy is successfully saving all of the data files required to perform tablespace, database and point-in-time recovery. Oracle worldwide support have experienced a high percentage of sites that could not recover all of the data lost in a critical failure because not all of the required files were backed up in the first place. If your backup strategy is ineffective it is better to find out during a practice recovery rather than finding out when your production system is down. Tests should include recovering from both physical and logical database errors.

We will look at how to recover your Oracle database using the SAPDBA utility together with other recovery mechanisms available in Oracle. It is not possible to use SAPDBA to recover from all types of failures you may encounter so we will show you how to recover in these situations.

6.1   R/3 recovery concepts

Knowing how to recover your failed R/3 system requires an understanding of how R/3 and Oracle work together. It also involves knowing where your data files, control files, online and archived redo logs are located. If you have read Chapter 3 – Oracle architecture and Chapter 4 – Configuring SAP R/3 and Oracle you will know where the critical Oracle files are and their importance to the R/3 system. Chapter 5 – SAP R/3 backup guide discussed what you should backup, why and how frequently.

The purpose of a recovery is to perform two operations: a *restore*, which is the process of copying the required files from tape back to disk, or simply locating the required files if they are already on disk; followed by a *recovery*, which is the process of setting the database back to a consistent state where all of the database files have the same internal timestamp. There are several types of recovery you may have to perform. A *full database recovery* which involves restoring the entire database from a backup, a *partial recovery* where one or more files will be restored, and a *point-in-time recovery* where the database is recovered to a point-in-time prior to the failure.

As discussed in previous sections, there are several mechanisms available to you for backing up your R/3 system. SAP supplies BRBACKUP, which will backup your data files, control files and online redo logs, together with BRARCHIVE which backs up your archived redo logs. We have also discussed the options you have available if you decide to backup your system using the Oracle supplied tools.

Depending on which tool(s) you have used to perform your backup, your recovery strategy will be different. We will consider how to recover using both the SAP and Oracle supplied tools. If you have used tools from a third party then you need to know how to restore your files using that tool. The recovery process will be similar to that described in this chapter.

When recovering a failed database you must be aware of any structural changes that may have taken place since the latest backup. A structural change can be the addition of a new tablespace, a new data file added to an existing tablespace, or new tables and/or indexes that may have been created. When these types of changes occur it is important to immediately backup the relevant tablespace, data file(s) and/or database objects, if you do not you are at risk of permanently losing the changes. You may even find that some third-party tools detect that a structural change has occurred to your database that was not backed up and may refuse to restore any files from the backup!

Before performing any type of recovery you must take the time to analyze what has gone wrong, what database objects have been affected, and why the failure has occurred. This analysis will provide you with the information you need to determine the type of recovery you need to perform, the tools you will use to perform the recovery, and will also help you avoid potentially corrupting your database further by restoring the wrong files from your backup. Oracle worldwide support can cite many real-life cases where the DBA tried to perform a recovery that was not appropriate for the type of database failure encountered, and which actually resulted in further loss of data. **Do not be tempted to try and recover without analyzing the situation first!** Later in this chapter we will discuss how you can analyze a variety of database failures and show you what type of recovery you need to perform based on your findings.

Database failures can be caused by one of the following situations:

- **Logical failures** – these types of failures can be caused by background processes, SQL statement errors, database objects that are inadvertently dropped, or software bugs which affect data integrity. If your R/3 system suffers a data integrity error then it can be hard to solve since the internal logical structure and relationship between the R/3 objects is very complex.

- **Hardware or media failures** – such as a disk head crash, file corruption or total failure of the database server. Usually these types of errors involve some element of recovery from a backup.

In the following sections we will look at how SAPDBA can be used to perform recovery and the requirements which you must meet in order to be able to successfully recover your database with this utility. We will also look at how you can analyze different types of failures using tools supplied with your Oracle database system and what recovery options are available.

6.2   R/3 recovery strategy

6.2.1   What recovery options are supported with SAPDBA?

SAPDBA can be used to perform full database and individual file restores and for performing full database recovery. This means that SAPDBA can be used to restore and recover any data files belonging to the R/3 tablespaces as well as the Oracle SYSTEM tablespace. A DBA can perform point-in-time recovery as well as restoring missing control files.

Some error conditions cannot be recovered with SAPDBA. These include the loss of all control files, structural database changes or defective online redo logs. In these cases the DBA must use an Oracle supplied tool, such as RMAN supplied with Oracle8, or Oracle's Enterprise Manager or Server Manager, as supplied with Oracle7.

6.2.2   Recovery requirements when using SAP utilities

You can only use SAPDBA to recover your database if the following requirements are met:

- The SAP utilities BRBACKUP and BRARCHIVE must have been used to perform the original backup. SAPDBA requires access to the logs to be able to determine what was backed up and to where. You must ensure that you do not delete these logs and you should also make sure that they are available on disk before starting the recovery. If they are archived to tape then you must restore them before you begin.

- You will require a backup copy of the database data files and a copy of all of the archived redo logs from the time of the backup to the time of the failure.

- You will require a copy of all of the control files (this includes the mirrored copies). There are normally three control files in a default R/3 installation.

- You will require a copy of one of the members of the online redo log groups.

If you are unable to meet either of the last two requirements you will need to perform your recovery using an Oracle supplied utility.

6.2.3   Diagnosing problems

Tracing events

In this section we will discuss the diagnostic facilities available in Oracle that can be used to diagnose problems when failures start to occur on the R/3 database. To be able to fully analyze a failure, and therefore be able to determine the recovery procedures to be used to recover from the failure, you may need to read trace files and dump the contents of files such as control files, redo logs and data file headers. Some of this information is useful to you to help solve error conditions, some of it is only useful to Oracle technical support and the Oracle development teams.

The starting point when any type of failure occurs is the Oracle alert log. This file can be found in the /oracle/<SID>/saptrace directory of a default R/3 installation. Oracle writes sequentially to this file, which contains a lot of useful information, including:

- the names of any trace files created by background and/or user processes;

- the status of the Oracle background processes;

- the initialization parameters that are currently in effect for the database;

- details of the online redo logs, including the current redo log sequence number being written to, together with details of all log switches;

- database startup and shutdown events;

- information regarding any database changes that have taken place such as tablespace creations, new rollback segments, some of the alter statements that have been executed such as ALTER TABLESPACE, for example.

Each message has a timestamp and those that are informative, as opposed to error, conditions will usually have a start time and an end time showing the successful completion of a particular action. It is important that you regularly check this file for any error conditions that may occur from time to time. Very often impending problems can be detected this way before they eventually bring the database down. An example alert log can be seen in Figure 6.1.

```
LICENSE_MAX_SESSION = 0
LICENSE_SESSIONS_WARNING = 0
LICENSE_MAX_USERS = 0
Starting up ORACLE RDBMS Version: 7.3.2.1.0.
System parameters with non-default values:
  processes                = 50
  control_files            =
/ora/app/oracle/oradata/P6Q_ORA/control01.ctl,
/ora/app/oracle/oradata/P6Q_ORA/control02.ctl,
/ora/app/oracle/oradata/P6Q_ORA/control03.ctl
  log_buffer               = 8192
  log_checkpoint_interval  = 10000
  db_files                 = 20
  rollback_segments        = r01, r02, r03, r04
```

Figure 6.1   Contents of an Oracle alert log file

```
    sequence_cache_hash_buckets= 10
    remote_login_passwordfile= NONE
    mts_service              = P6Q_ORA
    mts_servers              = 0
    mts_max_servers          = 0
    mts_max_dispatchers      = 0
    audit_trail              = NONE
    sort_area_retained_size  = 65536
    sort_direct_writes       = AUTO
    db_name                  = P6Q_ORA
    ifile                    =
/ora/app/oracle/admin/P6Q_ORA/pfile/configP6Q_ORA.ora
    background_dump_dest     = /ora/app/oracle/admin/P6Q_ORA/bdump
    user_dump_dest           = /ora/app/oracle/admin/P6Q_ORA/udump
    max_dump_file_size       = 10240
    core_dump_dest           = /ora/app/oracle/admin/P6Q_ORA/cdump
DBWR started
PMON started
LGWR started
Fri Oct 2 05:35:55 1998
alter database mount exclusive
Successful mount of redo thread 1.
Fri Oct 2 05:35:56 1998
Completed: alter database mount exclusive
Fri Oct 2 05:35:56 1998
alter database open
Fri Oct 2 05:35:57 1998
Thread 1 opened at log sequence 102
  Current log# 3 seq# 102 mem# 0:
/ora/app/oracle/oradata/P6Q_ORA/redoP6Q_ORA03.log
Successful open of redo thread 1.
Fri Oct 2 05:35:57 1998
SMON: enabling cache recovery
SMON: enabling tx recovery
Fri Oct 2 05:36:01 1998
Completed: alter database open
Fri Oct 2 05:48:58 1998
ALTER TABLESPACE USERS COALESCE
```

Figure 6.1   Continued

The second place to look when diagnosing problems are the trace files created by both the Oracle database background processes and user processes. The Oracle background processes always write trace files, even under normal operating conditions, so the presence of a trace file in this case does not mean you are experiencing a problem. User processes, on the other hand, only create trace files when they cannot successfully complete a user request or when the DBA has requested that a trace file be written for a particular user process by issuing the `ALTER SESSION` command. These trace files can be found in the same directory as the alert log. They are named according to the process ID of the process that created them. If an Oracle background process creates them they will also contain the Oracle ID of that process. By default all files end with the suffix '.trc'.

Before we look at how to analyze specific error conditions, let's examine how we can trace certain events.

How to trace events

The Oracle RDBMS has a facility that allows the DBA to dump information to trace files when a certain event occurs. Several of these events can be used to determine why failures are occurring in the R/3 database, can help to determine why your database appears to be hanging (freezing) for no apparent reason, and can provide valuable information about many other common problems.

There are two ways to turn on the tracing of such events. One way is to use the `EVENT` parameter in the Oracle initialization file, the second way is to dynamically set tracing on for a particular user by executing the `ALTER SESSION SET EVENTS` command from within Server Manager. The syntax to use when setting tracing from the `init<SID>.ora` file is:

```
EVENT = "<event>|, LEVEL <n>|:<event>|, LEVEL <n> etc...
```

For example `EVENT = "604 TRACE NAME ERRORSTACK FOREVER"` would turn on a trace to dump the contents of the errorstack every time an ORA-604 error was encountered.

To turn on the same trace dynamically from Server Manager you would execute the following command: `ALTER SESSION SET EVENTS '604 TRACE NAME ERRORSTACK FOREVER'`; whilst logged on to the database as the R/3 database schema owner.

The syntax of these commands is as follows:

- `<event>` defines the event you want to trace and consists of several parts. Firstly an event number, which can be either an Oracle error number (which is normally prefixed by ORA-), or an internal event code defined within the Oracle database kernel. The valid event codes that can be used are defined on UNIX in the file `oraus.msg`. We will discuss the ones that are the most useful to you later in this chapter. The event number can also be replaced with a special keyword `immediate`, which will cause Oracle to dump the required information to a trace file unconditionally. This keyword is only used as part of the `ALTER SESSION SET EVENTS` command as it does not make sense to define it in the initialization file. The next part of the `<event>` are the keywords `trace` and `name` followed by the name of the structure you want to trace. Other keywords are acceptable here but are only used as instructed by Oracle worldwide support. The third part is the length of time you want this trace to be active. If you are not using the immediate keyword, then you will normally specify forever, as in our previous example. This means the tracing will continue for the length of the user session (if set with the ALTER SESSION command) or until it is manually turned off (if defined in the init<SID>.ora file).

- LEVEL <n> defines the amount of information that should be dumped to the trace file. Be careful how you use this parameter as some events can dump a lot of information making the trace file very large. <n> can be in the range 1–10. The higher the number the more information that will be dumped. The highest number 10 will cause everything to be dumped to the trace file. A 1 will only dump the header information. Depending on the event name, LEVEL has a different meaning. If you are tracing block information then you can use LEVEL to define the decimal address of the actual block you want to trace. The address will be supplied to you by Oracle worldwide support and you should not use the block tracing events without their supervision.

- : separates multiple events if you want to turn more than one trace on at the same time. This syntax is also acceptable when using ALTER SESSION to turn on tracing.

Useful events to trace

There are a large number of events that can be traced, depending on the problem you are trying to analyze. There follows a list of the most useful events to trace when analyzing failures in an R/3 database. These events can be traced on both Oracle7 and Oracle8 databases.

CONTROLF – this event will cause the control file information to be dumped to a trace file. You should use this event to:

- check the status of the database data files;

- check the status of the online redo logs;

- see which redo log thread is currently open;

- see if the redo logs have been reset at any time during database startup (i.e. Oracle opened using the RESETLOGS parameter);

- check the version number of the database and redo log files. Occasionally a DBA may restore a data file or redo log file that is not consistent with the other files. This occurs when a data file or log file is restored from the wrong backup set. By dumping the contents of the control file you can immediately see which data file is causing the problem;

- find the full pathname of all the data files and log files when the database is down. This information can normally be found by querying the V$DATAFILE table but the database must be open or mounted which may not be possible after a catastrophic failure.

Use one of the following commands if you need to dump control file information.

To dump the entire contents of the control file:

```
alter session set events 'immediate trace name controlf level 10';
```

To dump only the control file header:

```
alter session set events 'immediate trace name controlf level 1';
```

You can also look at control file information by querying certain V$ views. This will be more efficient than setting the CONTROLF event. See the discussion later in this chapter in the section headed **V$ views**. We discuss how to analyze the contents of the control file later in this chapter.

   REDOHDR – this event will dump the header of the online redo logs. You should use this event if you receive error messages from Oracle stating that some data files have failed verification checks. Use this event in combination with the CONTROLF and FILE_HDRS events (explained later).

   To turn this trace on, use one of the following commands.

To dump the redo log file header as recorded in the control file:

```
alter session set events 'immediate trace name redohdr level 1';
```

To dump the contents of the header from the actual online redo log files:

```
alter session set events 'immediate trace name controlf level 10';
```

We discuss how to analyze the contents of the redo log file headers later in this chapter.

   FILE_HDRS – this event dumps the contents of the data file headers and is normally used when setting the REDOHDR trace. The setting for LEVEL is the same as described for REDOHDR.

To dump the contents of the data file headers as recorded in the control file:

```
alter session set events 'immediate trace name file_hdrs level 1';
```

To dump the contents of the header from the actual data files:

```
alter session set events 'immediate trace name file_hdrs level 10';
```

We discuss how to analyze the contents of the data file headers later in this chapter.

   SYSTEMSTATE – this event dumps the state of all processes running at the time of the dump. Use this trace if your system starts to experience any of the following:

- sudden performance degradation

- processes hanging for no apparent reason

- system hangs for no apparent reason.

Always use the following statement to turn this trace on:

```
alter session set events 'immediate trace name systemstate level 10';
```

We discuss how to use this information later in this chapter. **If you need to use this trace please contact Oracle technical support first**.

   ERRORSTACK – this event dumps all of the error messages stored on the internal error stack. Use this trace if R/3 receives an Oracle error and you think that there may be knock-on errors that have occurred and you want to see what these errors are in order to be able to fully understand the problem. You should only dump the error stack for the Oracle error of interest. For example, if R/3 receives an ORA-604 error then you would want to dump the error stack the next time this error occurs by executing this command:

```
alter session set events '604 trace name errorstack forever';
```

To dump the error stack for other Oracle errors simply replace '604' in the above command with the relevant 'ORA-' error number.

We discuss how to use this information later in this chapter.

LOCKS – is a useful trace if you are using the Oracle Parallel Server option (OPS) with R/3. In this configuration you may need to determine what locks are being held by the LCK background process especially if you are getting lock related errors. To turn on this trace use the following command:

```
alter session set events 'immediate trace name locks level 5';
```

The remaining events are all internal event codes as defined by Oracle and found in the `oraus.msg` file. **Please note that some of these codes may not be available in all versions of Oracle and that they may be de-supported by Oracle without notice. Also some of these codes should not be used without the supervision of Oracle technical support.**

It is advisable to try these events on your test system before using them on your production R/3 system.

10231 and **10232** – these are very useful event codes. Let's assume you have a situation where there has been a physical disk hardware failure such as a head crash and that this has caused some block corruption. To try and recover the remaining data from the affected table you use the Oracle Export utility. Oracle Export will perform a full table scan and when it reaches the corrupted block it will get an Oracle error reported and the Export will immediately stop. This means that you will not be able to retrieve the data beyond the corrupted block. In order to retrieve all of the data using Export you should set event 10231, which will cause Export to skip the corrupted blocks and continue reading the data. In this case you will only lose the data previously stored in the corrupted block. If you also set event 10232, each corrupted block found will be dumped to a trace file.

To set these events, use the following command:

```
event = "10231 trace name context forever, level 10:10232 trace name
context forever, level 10"
```

Notice that we are using the EVENT parameter that is defined in the `init<SID>.ora` initialization file. Oracle recommends using this parameter when dealing with block corruption problems.

In order for the above events to work correctly two additional conditions must be met:

- The corrupted block(s) must be marked as soft-corrupted by Oracle. To force Oracle to zero out certain parts of a block, thereby making it soft-corrupted, you must set event 10210 (see later for an explanation of this event code).

- Once you have set the above events in the `init<SID>.ora` file you must retrieve the data from the relevant table(s) using a full table scan. This can be achieved by using

either the Oracle Export utility, or using an SQL statement that performs a `SELECT *`
`FROM`. You will not be able to successfully bypass the corruption if an index is used.

10013 and **10015** – these event codes are used to diagnose rollback segment corruption
problems. You would normally use these codes if you were getting an ORA-1578 error.
This error tells you that you have block corruption somewhere in the database but does
not tell you which object is affected. If you suspect it is a rollback segment that is affected,
setting these event codes will tell you which rollback segment it is and will dump the corrupt segment to a trace file.

Use this command to enable these event codes:

```
event = "10013 trace name context forever:10015 trace name context
forever"
```

The author recommends you set these events in the Oracle initialization file.

10210 and **10211** – these are *block* checking and *index* checking event codes respectively.
When turned on these events will integrity check every data block and every index block
before it is read into the Oracle SGA (System Global Area). Oracle will mark any corrupted blocks it finds as *soft-corrupted* by zeroing out certain parts of the block. If event
code 10231 is also turned on you will be able to skip these corrupted blocks during table
scans. If your R/3 database is very large (greater than 20GB as defined by SAP), then
Oracle advise you permanently turn these events on **but there will be a significant overhead**. The Oracle background process PMON always performs block checking.

To turn these events on, use these commands.

For data block checking:

```
event = '10210 trace name context forever, level 10'
```

For index checking:

```
event = '10211 trace name context forever, level 10'
```

10061 – this event may need to be used after a database crash, or after the database has
been closed using the `shutdown abort` command. Event 10061 will prevent the Oracle
background process SMON from deleting temporary tables used during sorting. If these
tables are causing problems you may need to re-open the database without removing
them so that they can be analyzed by Oracle technical support.

This event should be turned on using the `EVENT` parameter in the initialization file and
turned off as soon as the problem has been resolved. This event code is available from
Oracle7 release 7.0.15 upwards.

Using **INIT.ORA** *Settings*

The following `init<SID>.ora` parameter is useful when debugging corruption problems:

`_DB_BLOCK_COMPUTE_CHECKSUMS`

This parameter has been documented by Oracle since version 7.2. This parameter should
be used if you suspect block corruptions are happening on disk. It will cause Oracle to

calculate a checksum for each block it reads from disk and it will write the checksum into the SGA along with the block itself. The next time Oracle reads the same block it will recompute the checksum and compare it. If it is found to be different it assumes the block has become corrupted, marks the block as such on disk, and signals an error. There is a significant overhead incurred when this parameter is used so only use it under guidance from Oracle technical support.

To set this parameter in the init<SID>.ora file enter this line:

```
_DB_BLOCK_COMPUTE_CHECKSUMS = true
```

R/3 locking problems

Earlier we discussed the enqueue work process that is responsible for managing the internal locking of database objects. This locking mechanism is provided in R/3 in addition to the locking capabilities provided by the Oracle RDBMS.

This locking mechanism enables R/3 to perform locking at a business function level rather than simply at a database object level. This means that:

- multiple database objects can be locked and treated as a single entity;

- in a client/server configuration where there are multiple application servers, each server is aware of the locks currently in place;

- all locks are valid system-wide;

- R/3 can run on multiple processor systems.

As R/3 lock entries are responsible for protecting data integrity it is the responsibility of the DBA to ensure they are functioning correctly and, on occasion, to manually release locks under abnormal conditions.

Normally locks are released automatically by R/3 when programs no longer require them. Occasionally this is not possible due to the fact that the dispatcher may not be able to release a lock. This can occur, for example, where users shutdown their PC without logging off of R/3. Frequent monitoring of the lock entries should be a regular maintenance task since unreleased locks reduce transaction throughput and can compromise data integrity.

To display and perform operations on lock entries go to the *Lock Entries* screen, which is accessed, from the *Tools → Administration → Monitoring → Lock Entries* menu in R/3. Lock entries can be selected by R/3 client number, user name, table name or lock argument. All lock entries can be viewed by entering the "*" wildcard parameter in both the client and user fields. By pressing the continue button a list of locks is displayed in tabular format. Each row relates to a lock entry and shows the R/3 client, the user holding the lock, the time the lock was granted, an indicator if the lock is shared, the name of the table with locked rows and the lock argument.

The purpose of monitoring these lock entries is to identify those locks which are being held for a long period of time. This may not always indicate a problem as you may have some long running transactions, but you should always be aware of this condition. Once you discover a problem you should always investigate the cause before manually deleting the lock using the features provided from the lock entries screen. If you have no alternative but to delete entries make sure that it will not affect an update work process, a background job or other users.

The main causes of unreleased locks are:

- **Abnormal termination of the SAPGUI client** – users terminating their connection abnormally without logging off cause this problem. For PC users this means they may have switched their machine off! Other reasons include a network connection failure. This can also affect the Oracle server process that is accessing the database on behalf of the terminated connection and may cause an abnormal increase in CPU cycles to occur. Since the user is no longer connected, the dispatcher process cannot automatically release the lock and therefore it will have to be deleted manually.

- **Inactive SAPGUI client** – this may cause a lock to be held for extended periods. This condition occurs when a user enters, or modifies data, but does not save (commit) the changes. In this situation other users requiring access to the same data will be held up and their session may freeze. The solution is to get the user to either save or discard the changes thereby releasing the lock. As a drastic measure the lock can again be deleted if it is causing serious bottlenecks in the system.

- **Problems with update processing** – as discussed earlier, R/3 processes updates in the background to allow maximum transaction throughput. The dispatcher will write update requests to a table in the database and then signal an update work process to perform the changes to the database. If there are update modules that are unprocessed in the system, locks will not be released. The only time they are released is if all update records have been successfully completed or the update work process terminates with an error status. From the lock entry screen you can distinguish update entries because they have the backup flag set. If you frequently get update lock entries that are not automatically released, you should try to determine the underlying problem. Whilst you are analyzing the problem it may be worth deactivating updating to avoid constant problems being reported back to users, causing them to have to re-enter the data for each failed update. By deactivating updates, all the transactions, including background processing, are paused and users are not allowed to initiate any more update requests. Once the update problem is solved and updates are reactivated, all paused processes will automatically resume and all locks should be automatically released.

- **Enqueue process problems** – the problems described so far assume that the locking mechanism is working correctly. There are situations where this may not be the case and therefore the whole enqueue locking process will be affected. From the lock entries screen there is an *Extras* menu option, which provides access to some useful diagnostic facilities to automatically pinpoint enqueue work process problems. The two most useful functions are the *Diagnosis* and *Diagnosis in update* options. These functions will test that the enqueue work process is functioning correctly, and allow an update test to be performed. Any problems found will be reported.

R/3 system logs

R/3 provides extensive logging facilities to record events and errors that occur during operation. The information to be found in the system logs is similar to that found in the Oracle alert log. When analyzing problems on R/3, the system log is always a good place to start.

R/3 allows two types of logs to be written. The default installation will have each application server in your SAP environment writing to its own *local log*. This log is stored within the specific instance directory for that application server which generically is:

```
/usr/sap/<SID>/<INSTANCE_NAME>/log
```

The log file name is SLOG followed by the R/3 instance number, therefore for an R/3 system with a SID K20 and an instance D03 the log file would be /usr/sap/K20/ D03/log/ SLOG03. Each application server writes its messages to a circular log file. When the log file reaches its maximum defined size (as specified by the system parameter rslg/max_diskspace/local) a log switch occurs and log messages are written from the beginning of the file again, overwriting the previous ones.

The alternative to each application server maintaining its own log, is to have one *central log* which contains the log records of all application servers in the one file. If you prefer this method of logging you must configure R/3 to specifically do this by changing the relevant parameter via transaction SM21. It is not possible to have central logging on NT machines. Figure 6.2 shows the process architecture for central logging of messages.

Central logging uses two files, an active and inactive one. When the active log file reaches the maximum defined size, a log switch occurs which causes the old inactive file to be deleted, copies the active one so that it now becomes the inactive one, and creates a

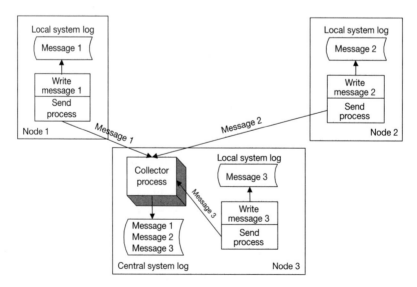

Figure 6.2   R/3 central system logging

new active log file. All of this occurs transparently to the administrator, not even an event is raised to indicate that a log switch has occurred. The maximum size of the *central log* is defined by the system parameter `rslg/max_diskspace/central` and the log can be found in the central directory `/usr/sap/<SID>/SYS/global`. The name of the inactive log file is normally `SLOG0`, whilst the active one is called `SLOGJ`. Both of these names can be changed via the system profile parameters.

To access the R/3 system logs either:

- execute transaction code `SM21`; or

- from the main CCMS menu select *Tools* → *Administration* → *Monitoring* → *System Log*; or

- from the performance menu select *Exceptions/Users* → *Exceptions* → *System Log*.

From the screen displayed it is possible to select filtering criteria to return the log records of interest. The criteria you can use include:

- *From date/To date* – allows a date range to be specified, which will return all log records timestamped between those dates.

- *User ID* – you can enter one of two values here: CPIC which will return log messages for R/3 instances initiated by other instances; SAPSYS which displays log messages for the background processing system.

- *Transaction code* – enter a transaction code to display all log messages relating to that transaction.

- *R/3 process* – this will display log messages for a particular work process. Valid values are:
    DP – for the dispatcher
    D<n> – to display messages for a particular work process number e.g. D1
    VB – for the updating processes messages
    V<n> – to display messages for a particular update work process
    S<n> – to display messages from the spool work process
    MS – for messages generated by the message server.

- *Problem classes* – allows you to select the type of messages you want to see such as errors, warnings, or, by default, all types.

- *Instance name* – this only appears if you have configured a central log. This field accepts the name of one of the R/3 instances.

- *Other options* – are available to allow you to format the output.

To view each application server's log from one central location go to the *System log* → *Choose* menu option. From here you can select the log type you want to view:

- *Local system log* – which is the default and allows you to view the log of the application server to which you are logged in.

- *Remote system log* – allows you to view logs from other application servers.

- *Central system log* – allows the central log to be viewed.

- *All remote system logs* – displays the log messages from all application server logs.

Each log entry displayed has a message code that indicates the type of log event. By double clicking on an event you will see an explanation of that event, and if it is an error, an explanation of the possible cause of the problem.

R/3 system traces

Apart from the system logs, R/3 includes facilities to debug and keep track of its internal operations. The tracing functions provided are primarily used for trying to resolve problems and to optimize the performance of ABAP/4 programs. Our discussion here is to help with problem solving and therefore our discussion is limited to the *System traces*. Other traces that are available are developer traces, SQL traces and ABAP/4 program traces. System tracing is accessed from the *Tools → Administration → Monitoring → Traces → System trace* menu. By selecting this menu option system tracing can be turned on and off. It is advisable to always have tracing turned on for each application server.

It is not obvious how you configure tracing so follow these steps in order to set and display system traces:

- Start the trace utility from the main menu *Tools → Administration → Monitoring → Traces → System trace*.

- From the main trace screen select the *Switch,edit* button and select the type of trace you want to see. You must also select the *Write to file* option so that the trace messages are written to disk.

- Select the *Standard options* button from the main trace screen and define what you want to trace.

- To start tracing, select the *Trace switch → Editor save → Inactive system* menu option. The trace will start recording all activities for the filter entered in the previous step.

- Once you have completed tracing you should stop the trace by going back to the session where you enabled the trace, select *Trace switch → Immediate switch → Stop trace* and wait a couple of minutes for the trace buffer to be written to disk.

- To display the trace file, go to the main trace screen and click on the *Standard* button. From here you will see a list of trace files.

- Double click on the trace file you require to display its contents.

- Double clicking on any of the trace messages will provide you with further information about that message. Some of the more technical messages may need further explanation, and in this case the author suggests you read the online documentation about tracing for help, or go to the SAPnet website at *http://sapnet.sap-ag.de* .

The system traces are written to circular files as specified in the *File selection* option from the *Switch,edit* button. If you do not specify a file selection the traces will be written to the same file, overwriting previous traces. These files are located in the

```
/usr/sap/<SID>/<INSTANCE_NAME>/log
```

directory and their names are TRACE<x><system number>. The <x> is substituted with the value entered in the *File selection* option and the <system number> is the R/3 instance number.

Before writing trace entries to disk they are written to a trace buffer in memory which is then transferred to disk when the buffer becomes full. This speeds up the trace process. Some trace files may contain entries for more than one trace; each one is marked so you can identify them. You can limit the maximum file size of the trace files using the system parameter rstr/max_diskspace. The location of the files is controlled by the *rstr/file* system parameter.

6.2.4   Debugging Oracle

Debug utilities

Oracle provide a debugger with both version 7 and 8 of the RDBMS. In releases 7.2 and below it is a separate executable called ORADBX, in later releases it is invoked from within the line mode version of Server Manager by entering the command oradebug.

In addition to these utilities there are various V$ tables that also provide useful debug information which we shall discuss here.

ORADBX

This program, available since version 6.0.29 up to and including release 7.2, allows the DBA to debug Oracle processes. It sends asynchronous messages to the active Oracle process so that trace information can be dumped for structures such as the SGA, PGA (Program Global Area), state objects, context area, stack trace, system states, control file, data file, ipc information and core. From this list it can be seen that some of this information can also be dumped using the EVENT parameter or the ALTER SESSION command. The advantage of using ORADBX is that it allows the DBA to turn on event traces for processes that are already running.

Figure 6.3 shows the help listing from the oradbx command. This list shows all the information that can be dumped to trace.

For example, to dump the process error buffer, call stack, process state and context area you would:

1. Find the process id of the process you want to dump trace information for using the UNIX ps command.
2. Start ORADBX.
3. Enter debug <pid> (substituting <pid> with the process id found in step 1).
4. Enter dump level 3.

The trace information would be written to a trace file.

```
(oradbx) help
help                          - print help information
show                          - show status
debug <pid>                   - debug process
dump SGA                      - dump SGA
dump PGA                      - dump PGA
dump stack                    - dump call stack
dump core                     - dump core without crashing process
dump level 0                  - dump error buffer
dump level 1                  - level 0 + call stack
dump level 2                  - level 1 + process state objects
dump level 3                  - level 2 + context area
dump system 1                 - brief system states dump
dump system 2                 - full system states dump
dump ipc                      - dump ipc information
dump controlfile #            - dump control file at level #
dump datafile #               - dump data file header at level #
dump procstat                 - dump process statistics
event <event-trace>           - turn on event trace
unlimit trace                 - unlimit the size of trace file
exit                          - exit this program
!                             - shell escape
```

Figure 6.3   ORADBX help

ORADEBUG

This facility is accessed from the line mode of Server Manager, it is not a separate executable. Like oradbx, the oradebug command allows trace information to be dumped from an already executing process. It also allows events to be enabled for these processes dynamically.

Figure 6.4 shows how to execute ORADEBUG in Oracle8 and also shows the output from the help command.

In order to dump the locking information for a process you would do the following:

- Attach to the required process (after finding the process id from the ps command) by entering oradebug setospid <n>. Replace <n> with the process id number.

- Enter oradebug unlimit. This sets the trace file size to unlimited.

- Enter oradebug event immediate trace name locks, level 5. This sets the lock dump event. Notice the same format is used when setting this via the ALTER SESSION command.

- Enter oradebug flush, which will write the trace output to a file.

```
SVRMGR>   oradebug help
HELP              [command]                 Describe one or all
                                            commands
SETMYPID                                    Debug current process
SETOSPID          <ospid>                   Set OS pid of process to
                                            debug
SETORAPID         <orapid> ['force']        Set Oracle pid of process
                                            to debug
DUMP              <dump_name> <level>       Invoke named dump
DUMPSGA           [bytes]                   Dump fixed SGA
DUMPLIST                                    Print a list of
                                            available dumps
EVENT             <text>                    Set trace event in process
SESSION_EVENT     <text>

DUMPVAR           <p|s|uga> <name> [level]  Print/dump fixed
                                            PGA/SGA/UGA variable
SETVAR            <p|s|uga> <name> <value>  Modify a fixed PGA/SGA/UGA
                                            variable
PEEK              <addr> <len> [level]      Print/dump memory
POKE              <addr> <len> <value>      Modify memory
WAKEUP            <orapid>                   Wake up Oracle process
SUSPEND                                     Suspend execution
RESUME                                      Resume execution
FLUSH                                       Flush pending writes to
                                            trace file
TRACEFILE_NAME                              Get name of trace file
CORE                                        Dump core without crashing
                                            process
IPC                                         Dump ipc information
UNLIMIT                                     Unlimit the size of the
                                            trace file
PROCSTAT                                    Dump process statistics
CALL              <func> [arg1] ... [argn]  Invoke function with
                                            arguments
SVRMGR>   oradebug setospid 2571;
Oracle pid: 9, Unix process pid: 2571, image: oraclevk803
SVRMGR>   oradebug unlimit
Statement processed.
SVRMGR>   oradebug event immediate trace name locks, level 5
Statement processed.
SVRMGR>   oradebug flush
Statement processed.
```

Figure 6.4   ORADEBUG usage

When using either of these debug utilities, do not dump trace information for the Oracle background processes because exiting from these utilities could kill the background process, stopping the Oracle database.

V$ *views*

Every Oracle DBA will know about the V$ dynamic performance tables that are maintained by Oracle. They are usually used by the DBA to monitor and improve performance of the database. They can also be useful as a means for viewing information about backups, control files, log files and data files. These 'internal' tables have a set of V_$ views created on top of them and are accessed via a set of public synonyms with the V$ prefix. The following V$ views are useful for analyzing backup and recovery information:

- V$ACCESS – list of locks currently held in the database.
- V$BGPROCESS – information about the Oracle background processes.
- V$DATAFILE – information about the database data files.
- V$LOCK – information about non-DDL locks and resources.
- V$LOG – information about the redo logs (taken from the control file).
- V$LOGFILE – information about the redo log files.
- V$PROCESS – a list of the currently active processes.
- V$ROLLNAME – maps internal numbers of rollback segments to their externalized names.
- V$ROLLSTAT – information on the status of the online rollback segments.
- V$SESSION – the currently active sessions.
- V$SESSION_CONNECT_INFO – information on network connections for active sessions.
- V$SESSION_WAIT – list of resources or events for which session is waiting.
- V$THREAD – information about redo log threads (taken from the control file).
- V$BACKUP – information on the backup status of all online data files.
- V$BACKUP_CORRUPTION – information about corruptions in data file backups (taken from the control file).
- V$ARCHIVED_LOG – information about archived redo logs.
- V$BACKUP_DATAFILE – information on backup data files and backup control files (taken from the control file).
- V$BACKUP_DEVICE – list of available supported backup devices (disk is not listed here as it is assumed that it is always available).
- V$BACKUP_PIECE – information about backup pieces as stored in the control file. When backups are taken using RMAN, a backup set will contain more than one piece. This view contains a list of these pieces and which backup device they reside on.

- V$BACKUP_REDOLOG – information about archived redo log backup pieces stored in the control file. Data will only be available if you use RMAN to backup your archived redo logs.

- V$BACKUP_SET – list of all RMAN backup sets stored in the control file.

- V$CONTROLFILE – lists the names of all control files.

- V$CONTROLFILE_RECORD_SECTION – lists the location of each control file record as stored in the control file. See the explanation of control file dumps later in this chapter.

- V$COPY_CORRUPTION – contains information about data file copy corruptions as stored in the control file. This is the list of corruptions that occur when using the RMAN COPY command.

- V$DATABASE – contains database information as stored in the control file.

- V$DATAFILE_COPY – information about data files copied via the RMAN COPY command.

- V$DATAFILE_HEADER – contains header information for all data files.

- V$LOG_HISTORY – contains redo log history information taken from the control file.

- V$RECOVERY_LOG – contains a list of archived redo logs that are required to complete media recovery.

- V$RECOVER_FILE – contains the status of files needing media recovery.

- V$RECOVERY_FILE_STATUS – contains the status of each data file currently being recovered.

- V$RECOVERY_STATUS – contains information about the current recovery process.

Understanding control file dumps

As we discussed earlier, you may need to dump the contents of the control file in order to determine how to perform a recovery of your database. The control file can be dumped using the ALTER SESSION command. Depending on the problem you are trying to solve, it may be more convenient to view sections of the control file by querying one of the V$ views provided for this purpose, especially if you know in advance what section of the control file you need to see. The previous section highlighted the appropriate views you can use.

If you need to view any part of the control file it is important you understand how the control file is structured and what it can tell you to help with recovery. The structure of the control file changed from Oracle7 to Oracle8 so we will discuss these changes separately.

The Oracle7 control file

The control file is split into several sections as follows:

- control file header information
- database entry

- redo thread entries

- log file entries

- database file entries

- log file history entries.

Each section can provide useful information when debugging database failures. Figure 6.5 shows the contents of an Oracle7 control file. We shall refer to this figure throughout our following discussion by referencing the line numbers added by the author for ease of reference.

```
 1. Dump file
    /ora/app/oracle/admin/P6Q_ORA/udump/p6q_ora_ora_457.trc
 2. Oracle7 Server Release 7.3.2.1.0 - Production Release
 3. With the parallel query option
 4. PL/SQL Release 2.3.2.0.0 - Production
 5. ORACLE_HOME = /ora/app/oracle/product/7.3.2
 6. System name: SunOS
 7. Node name: ptchp6q
 8. Release: 5.5.1
 9. Version: Generic
10.Machine: sun4m
11.Instance name: P6Q_ORA
12.Redo thread mounted by this instance: 1
13.Oracle process number: 7
14.Unix process pid: 457, image: oracleP6Q_ORA
15.Sat Jan 16 09:14:05 1999
16.*** SESSION ID:(5.38) 1999.01.16.09.14.05.000
17.DUMP OF CONTROL FILES, Seq # 406 = 0x196
18.FILE HEADER:
19.Software vsn=117489664=0x700c000, Compatibility
   Vsn=117477376=0x7009000
20.Db Id=754995808=0x2d005260, Db Name='P6Q_ORA'
21.Control Seq=406=0x196, Creation file size=0=0x0 Current file
   size=216=0xd8
22.File Number=0, Blksiz=512, File Type=1
23.DATABASE ENTRY:
24.(offset = 0x200, size = 144, max = 1, hi = 1)
25.DF Version: creation=0x700c000 compatible=0x700b000, Date
   01/12/98 18:51:12
26.DB Name "P6Q_ORA"
27.Database flags = 0x00000000
```

Figure 6.5   Contents of an Oracle control file

```
28.Incmplt recovery scn: 0x0000.00000000 Resetlogs scn:
   0x0000.00000000 count: 0x0
29.Redo Version: creation=0x700c000 compatible=0x700c000
30.#Data files = 9, #Online files = 9
31.Database checkpoint: Thread=1 scn: 0x0000.000038e8
32.Threads: #Enabled=1, #Open=1, Head=1, Tail=1
33.enabled threads: 01000000 00000000 00000000 00000000 00000000
   00000000 00000000 00000000
34.Max log members = 2, Max data members = 1
35.Log hist = 101, Arch list: Head=0, Tail=0, Force scn:
   0x0000.00003736
36.REDO THREAD ENTRIES:
37.(offset = 0x290, size = 92, max = 8, hi = 1)
38.THREAD #1 - status:0x7 thread links forward:0 back:0
39.#logs:3 first:1 last:3 current:3 last used seq#:0x66
40.enabled at scn: 0x0000.00000001 01/12/98 18:51:14
41.opened at 01/16/99 08:38:06 by instance P6Q_ORA
42.Checkpointed at scn: 0x0000.000038e8 01/16/99 08:38:06
43.thread:1 rba:(0x66.3c9.10)
44.enabled threads: 01000000 00000000 00000000 00000000 00000000
   00000000 00000000 00000000
45.Archived entries: 101
46.LOG FILE ENTRIES:
47.(offset = 0x570, size = 72, max = 32, hi = 3)
48.LOG FILE #1:
49.(name #1) /ora/app/oracle/oradata/P6Q_ORA/redoP6Q_ORA01.log
50.Thread 1 redo log links: forward: 2 backward: 0
51.siz: 0x3e8 seq: 0x00000064 hws: 0x9 bsz: 512 nab: 0x3e6 flg:
   0x0 dup: 1
52.Archive links: fwrd: 0 back: 0 Prev scn: 0x0000.0000362d
53.Low scn: 0x0000.00003736 09/15/98 10:01:58
54.Next scn: 0x0000.00003794 09/22/98 06:13:48
55.LOG FILE #2:
56.(name #2) /ora/app/oracle/oradata/P6Q_ORA/redoP6Q_ORA02.log
57.Thread 1 redo log links: forward: 3 backward: 1
58.siz: 0x3e8 seq: 0x00000065 hws: 0x6 bsz: 512 nab: 0x3e9 flg:
   0x0 dup: 1
59.Archive links: fwrd: 0 back: 0 Prev scn: 0x0000.00003736
60.Low scn: 0x0000.00003794 09/22/98 06:13:48
61.Next scn: 0x0000.000037df 09/22/98 06:29:58
62.LOG FILE #3:
63.(name #3) /ora/app/oracle/oradata/P6Q_ORA/redoP6Q_ORA03.log
```

Figure 6.5　Continued

```
64.Thread 1 redo log links: forward: 0 backward: 2
65.siz: 0x3e8 seq: 0x00000066 hws: 0xd bsz: 512 nab: 0xffffffff
   flg: 0x8 dup: 1
66.Archive links: fwrd: 0 back: 0 Prev scn: 0x0000.00003794
67.Low scn: 0x0000.000037df 09/22/98 06:29:58
68.Next scn: 0xffff.ffffffff 09/15/98 10:01:58
69.DB FILE ENTRIES:
70.(offset = 0xe70, size = 132, max = 30, hi = 9)
71.DATA FILE #1:
72.(name #4) /ora/app/oracle/oradata/P6Q_ORA/system01.dbf
73.creation size=20480 block size=2048 status=0xf head=4 tail=4
   dup=1
74.Checkpoint cnt:144 scn: 0x0000.000038e8 stop scn:
   0xffff.ffffffff 10/02/98 11:58:08
75.Creation Checkpointed at scn: 0x0000.00000003 01/12/98 18:51:29
76.thread:1 rba:(0x1.3.10)
77.enabled threads: 01000000 00000000 00000000 00000000 00000000
   00000000 00000000 00000000
78.Offline scn: 0x0000.00000000
79.Online Checkpointed at scn: 0x0000.00000000 01/01/88 00:00:00
80.thread:0 rba:(0x0.0.0)
81.enabled threads: 00000000 00000000 00000000 00000000 00000000
   00000000 00000000 00000000
82.Hot Backup end marker scn: 0x0000.00000000
83.DATA FILE #2:
84.(name #5) /ora/app/oracle/oradata/P6Q_ORA/rbs01.dbf
85.creation size=4096 block size=2048 status=0xe head=5 tail=5
   dup=1
86.Checkpoint cnt:124 scn: 0x0000.000038e8 stop scn:
   0xffff.ffffffff 10/02/98 11:58:08
87.Creation Checkpointed at scn: 0x0000.0000117b 01/12/98 18:54:32
88.thread:1 rba:(0x14.39.10)
89.enabled threads: 01000000 00000000 00000000 00000000 00000000
   00000000 00000000 00000000
90.Offline scn: 0x0000.00000000
91.Online Checkpointed at scn: 0x0000.00000000 01/01/88 00:00:00
92.thread:0 rba:(0x0.0.0)
93.enabled threads: 00000000 00000000 00000000 00000000 00000000
   00000000 00000000 00000000
94.Hot Backup end marker scn: 0x0000.00000000
95.DATA FILE #3:
96.(name #6) /ora/app/oracle/oradata/P6Q_ORA/temp01.dbf
```

Figure 6.5   Continued

```
97.creation size=275 block size=2048 status=0xe head=6 tail=6
   dup=1
98.Checkpoint cnt:124 scn: 0x0000.000038e8 stop scn:
   0xffff.ffffffff 10/02/98 11:58:08
99.Creation Checkpointed at scn: 0x0000.00001180 01/12/98 18:54:33
100.  thread:1 rba:(0x14.40.10)
101.  enabled threads: 01000000 00000000 00000000 00000000
      00000000 00000000 00000000 00000000
102.  Offline scn: 0x0000.00000000
103.  Online Checkpointed at scn: 0x0000.00000000 01/01/88 00:00:00
104.  thread:0 rba:(0x0.0.0)
105.  enabled threads: 00000000 00000000 00000000 00000000
      00000000 00000000 00000000 00000000
106.  Hot Backup end marker scn: 0x0000.00000000
107.  DATA FILE #4:
108.  (name #7) /ora/app/oracle/oradata/P6Q_ORA/tools01.dbf
109.  creation size=7680 block size=2048 status=0xe head=7 tail=7
      dup=1
110.  Checkpoint cnt:124 scn: 0x0000.000038e8 stop scn:
      0xffff.ffffffff 10/02/98 11:58:08
111.  Creation Checkpointed at scn: 0x0000.00001185 01/12/98
      18:54:38
112.  thread:1 rba:(0x14.47.10)
113.  enabled threads: 01000000 00000000 00000000 00000000
      00000000 00000000 00000000 00000000
114.  Offline scn: 0x0000.00000000
115.  Online Checkpointed at scn: 0x0000.00000000 01/01/88 00:00:00
116.  thread:0 rba:(0x0.0.0)
117.  enabled threads: 00000000 00000000 00000000 00000000
      00000000 00000000 00000000 00000000
118.  Hot Backup end marker scn: 0x0000.00000000
119.  DATA FILE #5:
120.  (name #8) /ora/app/oracle/oradata/P6Q_ORA/users01.dbf
121.  creation size=512 block size=2048 status=0xe head=8 tail=8
      dup=1
122.  Checkpoint cnt:124 scn: 0x0000.000038e8 stop scn:
      0xffff.ffffffff 10/02/98 11:58:08
123.  Creation Checkpointed at scn: 0x0000.0000118b 01/12/98
      18:54:39
124.  thread:1 rba:(0x14.52.10)
125.  enabled threads: 01000000 00000000 00000000 00000000
      00000000 00000000 00000000 00000000
```

Figure 6.5   Continued

```
126.   Offline scn: 0x0000.00000000
127.   Online Checkpointed at scn: 0x0000.00000000 01/01/88 00:00:00
128.   thread:0 rba:(0x0.0.0)
129.   enabled threads: 00000000 00000000 00000000 00000000
       00000000 00000000 00000000 00000000
130.   Hot Backup end marker scn: 0x0000.00000000
131.   DATA FILE #6:
132.   (name #9) /app/oradata/autodata01.dbs
133.   creation size=30720 block size=2048 status=0xe head=9 tail=9
       dup=1
134.   Checkpoint cnt:83 scn: 0x0000.000038e8 stop scn:
       0xffff.ffffffff 10/02/98 11:58:08
135.   Creation Checkpointed at scn: 0x0000.00001bad 01/13/98
       23:05:20
136.   thread:1 rba:(0x3f.1ba.10)
137.   enabled threads: 01000000 00000000 00000000 00000000
       00000000 00000000 00000000 00000000
138.   Offline scn: 0x0000.00000000
139.   Online Checkpointed at scn: 0x0000.00000000 01/01/88 00:00:00
140.   thread:0 rba:(0x0.0.0)
141.   enabled threads: 00000000 00000000 00000000 00000000
       00000000 00000000 00000000 00000000
142.   Hot Backup end marker scn: 0x0000.00000000
143.   DATA FILE #7:
144.   (name #10) /app/oradata/autoindexes01.dbs
145.   creation size=10240 block size=2048 status=0xe head=10
       tail=10 dup=1
146.   Checkpoint cnt:83 scn: 0x0000.000038e8 stop scn:
       0xffff.ffffffff 10/02/98 11:58:08
147.   Creation Checkpointed at scn: 0x0000.00001bb2 01/13/98
       23:06:10
148.   thread:1 rba:(0x3f.1c1.10)
149.   enabled threads: 01000000 00000000 00000000 00000000
       00000000 00000000 00000000 00000000
150.   Offline scn: 0x0000.00000000
151.   Online Checkpointed at scn: 0x0000.00000000 01/01/88 00:00:00
152.   thread:0 rba:(0x0.0.0)
153.   enabled threads: 00000000 00000000 00000000 00000000
       00000000 00000000 00000000 00000000
154.   Hot Backup end marker scn: 0x0000.00000000
155.   DATA FILE #8:
156.   (name #11) /app/oradata/DbhHist01.dbs
```

Figure 6.5   Continued

```
157.  creation size=12800 block size=2048 status=0xe head=11
      tail=11 dup=1
158.  Checkpoint cnt:74 scn: 0x0000.000038e8 stop scn:
      0xffff.ffffffff 10/02/98 11:58:08
159.  Creation Checkpointed at scn: 0x0000.00001f19 01/14/98
      18:26:49
160.  thread:1 rba:(0x46.248.10)
161.  enabled threads: 01000000 00000000 00000000 00000000
      00000000 00000000 00000000 00000000
162.  Offline scn: 0x0000.00000000
163.  Online Checkpointed at scn: 0x0000.00000000 01/01/88 00:00:00
164.  thread:0 rba:(0x0.0.0)
165.  enabled threads: 00000000 00000000 00000000 00000000
      00000000 00000000 00000000 00000000
166.  Hot Backup end marker scn: 0x0000.00000000
167.  DATA FILE #9:
168.  (name #12) /app/oradata/DbhIdx01.dbs
169.  creation size=10240 block size=2048 status=0xe head=12
      tail=12 dup=1
170.  Checkpoint cnt:74 scn: 0x0000.000038e8 stop scn:
      0xffff.ffffffff 10/02/98 11:58:08
171.  Creation Checkpointed at scn: 0x0000.00001f1e 01/14/98
      18:26:58
172.  thread:1 rba:(0x46.24e.10)
173.  enabled threads: 01000000 00000000 00000000 00000000
      00000000 00000000 00000000 00000000
174.  Offline scn: 0x0000.00000000
175.  Online Checkpointed at scn: 0x0000.00000000 01/01/88 00:00:00
176.  thread:0 rba:(0x0.0.0)
177.  enabled threads: 00000000 00000000 00000000 00000000
      00000000 00000000 00000000 00000000
178.  Hot Backup end marker scn: 0x0000.00000000
179.  LOG FILE HISTORY ENTRIES:
180.  (offset = 0x8050, size = 28, max = 800, hi = 101)
181.  Earliest log history:
182.  Record 1: Thread=1 Seq#=1 Link=1
183.  Low scn: 0x0000.00000001 01/12/98 18:51:14 Next scn:
      0x0000.0000005e
184.  Latest log history:
185.  Record 101: Thread=1 Seq#=101 Link=100
186.  Low scn: 0x0000.00003794 09/22/98 06:13:48 Next scn:
      0x0000.000037df
187.  *** END OF DUMP ***
```

Figure 6.5   Continued

Control file header information

The first 17 lines are not part of the control file, they are the trace file header information which shows the version of Oracle the trace was run against, the process which created the trace together with a timestamp. The control file header begins proper at line 18. The following line shows the Oracle software version as a hexadecimal number. This is the Oracle version **that the control file was created under**; it may be different from the actual Oracle version (as indicated in the trace file header) if the software was updated since the control file was created. The compatible parameter indicates the lowest version of Oracle with which the format of this control file is compatible. The next line, line 20, shows the internal Db Id number generated at database creation time by combining the hashed Db Name and creation date. This internal id is written to all file headers for this database and is verified by Oracle every time the database is opened.

Line 21 shows the number of times the control file has been updated (*Control Seq*); this can therefore be considered the version number of the control file. On the same line we have the size of the control file shown in blocks not bytes. The first number is the decimal value, the second number is the hex value. These values do not include the header block and must be multiplied by the block size, shown in the following line, to give the control file size in bytes. Line 22 simply indicates that this is a control file (*File Type=1*).

Database entry

This section of the control file shows information regarding the database and in our example starts at line 23. The following line shows the offset, in hexadecimal, of where the database entry starts in the control file. This line also shows the size of the section in bytes. This enables any process reading this file to know where the section stops. Line 28 is important to the DBA because it shows if the database was opened with the RESETLOGS parameter. If this is the case, the *Incmplt recovery scn* will be non-zero and the *Resetlogs scn* will show the System Change Number (SCN) at which the database was opened. We will explain how Oracle uses the SCN during recovery later in this chapter. What is important to understand at this stage is that any changes that took place **before** this SCN cannot be recovered, which is why Oracle strongly recommends the DBA performs a full database backup when opening the database with RESETLOGS.

Line 30 shows the total number of data files that belong to the database, the *#Online files* parameter shows how many of these are online. Any files that are dropped from the database using the DROP TABLESPACE command are not included in these figures. Line 31 shows the SCN value at the last checkpoint, this value is used to determine which redo records need to be applied during recovery. Line 32 indicates the total number of threads that are enabled and open. If the *#Open* value is greater than one, then the database is running with the Parallel Server option. Line 34 shows the maximum number of log file members allowed per group followed by the maximum number of data file members per group. This last parameter will currently always be one because Oracle does not yet allow mirroring of data files. This is reserved for future implementation. The last line in this section (line 35) shows the last log history record in the control file. The important parameter here is the *Force scn* value. This determines which redo log is archived. Any redo that has an SCN before this value will be archived.

Redo thread entries

This section starts at line 36 and shows, for each redo thread that is enabled, the SCN value the time this thread was opened, the date and time it was opened and the SCN value at the checkpoint. The most important line in this section is line 39 which shows the number of log file groups that this thread contains (*#logs*) and the *current* log that the LGWR background process is writing to.

Log file entries

This section begins at line 46. Line 47 shows the offset information and the total number of log file groups, indicated by the *hi* parameter. The full path name of each redo log file is given at the beginning of each redo entry. The two important lines in this section are 53 and 54. These show the *Low scn* and *Next scn* values respectively. If this is the current online log that LGWR is writing to the *Next scn* will be set to infinity (in hex). In this case the *nab* parameter (line 51) shows the next available block that LGWR can use. When a log switch occurs, the high SCN of the previous log file becomes the low SCN of the next log file and the high SCN of the new log file is set to infinite.

Database file entries

This section gives details of all the database files. The *hi* parameter (line 70) shows the total number of data files in the database. For each data file, the full path is shown together with SCN information used for recovery purposes.

The *Checkpoint cnt* shows the number of times the data file has been checkpointed and this number continues to increment at every checkpoint even when the data file is in hot backup mode. The *stop scn* is the SCN after which no recovery is required for this file during data file recovery. Oracle will keep applying redo records until this number is reached. This number is only set when the database is shutdown normally, while the database is open it is set to infinity. Line 75 shows the *Creation Checkpointed at scn* value that is the SCN at the time this data file was created. Oracle records this so that it can rebuild the data file when the DBA executes the ALTER DATABASE CREATE DATAFILE command. This command allows the DBA to recreate a data file that was lost or damaged for which there was no backup, and to apply redo log entries to recreate the data within it. The redo entries that Oracle will start with are those indicated in the *Creation Checkpointed at scn* parameter. The *Offline scn* at line 78 is the SCN at the time the data file was taken offline. If the data file is part of the SYSTEM tablespace the value will always be zero because this tablespace cannot be taken offline.

The *Online Checkpointed at scn* value (line 79) is updated when the tablespace is put into backup mode using the `ALTER TABLESPACE BEGIN BACKUP` command prior to performing a hot backup of the data files. This will be updated for every data file in the tablespace.

Log file history entries

This is the last section of the Oracle7 control file and shows the log file history records. When you set the `CONTROLF` event and specify `LEVEL 10`, then the log history table will be dumped to trace. Please note, however, that not all of the entries will be dumped – only the first and last (as can be seen from line 181 onwards). To see all of these records query the `V$LOG_HISTORY` view. If the database is not open then set the `LOGHIST` event using an appropriate level. If the `LEVEL` is set to 1 it will dump the first and last log entries, if `LEVEL` is set to 2 or higher then the number of log entries dumped will be `2**LEVEL` (or 2 to the power `LEVEL`). For example:

```
alter session set events 'immediate trace name loghist level 5';
```

will dump 2**5 = 32 log history records. By the way, they will be the 32 *latest* records from the control file.

Line 180 shows the *max* number of log file entries that can be held in the control file, *hi* shows the number we currently have. When the maximum is reached the oldest entries will be overwritten.

The Oracle8 control file

In this section we will discuss the differences to be found in the Oracle8 control file. Figure 6.6 shows an example.

```
 1. Dump file /oracle/app/admin/ORA8DB/udump/ora8db_ora_492.trc
 2. Oracle8 Enterprise Edition Release 8.0.3.0.0 - Production
 3. With the Partitioning and Objects options
 4. PL/SQL Release 8.0.3.0.0 - Production
 5. ORACLE_HOME = /oracle/app/product/8.0.3
 6. System name: SunOS
 7. Node name:    ptchp6q
 8. Release:     5.5.1
 9. Version:    Generic
10.Machine:     sun4m
11.Instance name: ORA8DB
12.Redo thread mounted by this instance: 1
13.Oracle process number: 8
```

Figure 6.6   Contents of an Oracle8 control file

```
14.Unix process pid: 492, image: oracleORA8DB
15.Sat Jan 16 09:50:09 1999
16.*** SESSION ID:(9.22) 1999.01.16.09.50.09.000
17.DUMP OF CONTROL FILES, Seq # 1449 = 0x5a9
18.FILE HEADER:
19.Software vsn=134217728=0x8000000, Compatibility
   Vsn=134217728=0x8000000
20.Db Id=2887985999=0xac232b4f, Db Name='ORA8DB'
21.Control Seq=1449=0x5a9, File size=698=0x2ba
22.File Number=0, Blksiz=2048, File Type=1
23.DATABASE ENTRY:
24.(blkno = 0x1, size = 192, max = 1, in-use = 1, last-recid= 0)
25.DF Version: creation=0x8000000 compatible=0x8000000, Date
   01/16/98 15:52:47
26.DB Name "ORA8DB"
27.Database flags = 0x00004000
28.Controlfile Creation Timestamp 01/16/98 15:52:50
29.Incmplt recovery scn: 0x0000.00000000
30.Resetlogs scn: 0x0000.00000001 Resetlogs Timestamp 01/16/98
   15:52:47
31.Prior resetlogs scn: 0x0000.00000000 Prior resetlogs Timestamp
   01/01/88 00:00:00
32.Redo Version: creation=0x8000000 compatable=0x8000000
33.#Data files = 5, #Online files = 5
34.Database checkpoint: Thread=1 scn: 0x0000.000047aa
35.Threads: #Enabled=1, #Open=1, Head=1, Tail=1
36.enabled threads: 01000000 00000000 00000000 00000000 00000000
   00000000 00000000 00000000
37.Max log members = 2, Max data members = 1
38.Arch list: Head=0, Tail=0, Force scn: 0x0000.000046d4
39.Controlfile Checkpointed at scn: 0x0000.000047aa 01/01/88
   00:00:00
40.thread:0 rba:(0x0.0.0)
41.enabled threads: 00000000 00000000 00000000 00000000 00000000
   00000000 00000000 00000000
42.CHECKPOINT PROGRESS RECORDS:
43.(blkno = 0x6, size = 104, max = 8, in-use = 1, last-recid= 0)
44.THREAD #1 - status:0x2 flags:0x0 dirty:0
45.low cache rba:(0xffffffff.ffffffff.ffff) on disk
   rba:(0x1d4.316.0)
46.on disk scn: 0x0000.000047b2 01/16/99 08:38:49
47.THREAD #2 - status:0x0 flags:0x0 dirty:0
```

Figure 6.6   Continued

```
48.low cache rba:(0x0.0.0) on disk rba:(0x0.0.0)
49.on disk scn: 0x0000.00000000 01/01/88 00:00:00
50.THREAD #3 - status:0x0 flags:0x0 dirty:0
51.low cache rba:(0x0.0.0) on disk rba:(0x0.0.0)
52.on disk scn: 0x0000.00000000 01/01/88 00:00:00
53.THREAD #4 - status:0x0 flags:0x0 dirty:0
54.low cache rba:(0x0.0.0) on disk rba:(0x0.0.0)
55.on disk scn: 0x0000.00000000 01/01/88 00:00:00
56.THREAD #5 - status:0x0 flags:0x0 dirty:0
57.low cache rba:(0x0.0.0) on disk rba:(0x0.0.0)
58.on disk scn: 0x0000.00000000 01/01/88 00:00:00
59.THREAD #6 - status:0x0 flags:0x0 dirty:0
60.low cache rba:(0x0.0.0) on disk rba:(0x0.0.0)
61.on disk scn: 0x0000.00000000 01/01/88 00:00:00
62.THREAD #7 - status:0x0 flags:0x0 dirty:0
63.low cache rba:(0x0.0.0) on disk rba:(0x0.0.0)
64.on disk scn: 0x0000.00000000 01/01/88 00:00:00
65.THREAD #8 - status:0x0 flags:0x0 dirty:0
66.low cache rba:(0x0.0.0) on disk rba:(0x0.0.0)
67.on disk scn: 0x0000.00000000 01/01/88 00:00:00
68.REDO THREAD RECORDS:
69.(blkno = 0x6, size = 104, max = 8, in-use = 1, last-recid= 0)
70.THREAD #1 - status:0x7 thread links forward:0 back:0
71.#logs:3 first:1 last:3 current:3 last used seq#:0x1d4
72.enabled at scn: 0x0000.00000001 01/16/98 15:52:52
73.disabled at scn: 0x0000.00000000 01/01/88 00:00:00
74.opened at 01/16/99 08:38:45 by instance ORA8DB
75.Checkpointed at scn: 0x0000.000047aa 01/16/99 08:38:45
76.thread:1 rba:(0x1d4.305.10)
77.enabled threads: 01000000 00000000 00000000 00000000 00000000
    00000000 00000000 00000000
78.log history: 467
79.LOG FILE RECORDS:
80.(blkno = 0x7, size = 72, max = 32, in-use = 3, last-recid= 3)
81.LOG FILE #1:
82.(name #1) /ifx/oradata1/oradata/ORA8DB/redoORA8DB01.log
83.Thread 1 redo log links: forward: 2 backward: 0
84.siz: 0x3e8 seq: 0x000001d2 hws: 0x8 bsz: 512 nab: 0x3e9 flg: 0x0
    dup: 1
85.Archive links: fwrd: 0 back: 0 Prev scn: 0x0000.000046c7
86.Low scn: 0x0000.000046d4 01/16/98 16:34:08
87.Next scn: 0x0000.000046e3 01/16/98 16:34:13
```

Figure 6.6   Continued

```
88.LOG FILE #2:
89.(name #2) /app/oradata2/oradata/ORA8DB/redoORA8DB02.log
90.Thread 1 redo log links: forward: 3 backward: 1
91.siz: 0x3e8 seq: 0x000001d3 hws: 0x8 bsz: 512 nab: 0x3e9 flg:
   0x0 dup: 1
92.Archive links: fwrd: 0 back: 0 Prev scn: 0x0000.000046d4
93.Low scn: 0x0000.000046e3 01/16/98 16:34:13
94.Next scn: 0x0000.00004724 01/16/98 16:35:07
95.LOG FILE #3:
96.(name #3) /ora/oradata3/oradata/ORA8DB/redoORA8DB03.log
97.Thread 1 redo log links: forward: 0 backward: 2
98.siz: 0x3e8 seq: 0x000001d4 hws: 0x13 bsz: 512 nab: 0xffffffff
   flg: 0x8 dup: 1
99.Archive links: fwrd: 0 back: 0 Prev scn: 0x0000.000046e3
100.   Low scn: 0x0000.00004724 01/16/98 16:35:07
101.   Next scn: 0xffff.ffffffff 01/16/98 16:34:08
102.   DATA FILE RECORDS:
103.   (blkno = 0x9, size = 180, max = 30, in-use = 5, last-recid=
   5)
104.   DATA FILE #1:
105.   (name #4) /ifx/oradata1/oradata/ORA8DB/system01.dbf
106.   creation size=40960 block size=2048 status=0xe head=4 tail=4
   dup=1
107.   tablespace 0, index=1 krfil=1 prev_file=0
108.   unrecoverable scn: 0x0000.00000000 01/01/88 00:00:00
109.   Checkpoint cnt:480 scn: 0x0000.000047aa 01/16/99 08:38:45
110.   Stop scn: 0xffff.ffffffff 09/15/98 12:24:33
111.   Creation Checkpointed at scn: 0x0000.00000003 01/16/98
   15:53:37
112.   thread:1 rba:(0x1.3.10)
113.   enabled threads: 01000000 00000000 00000000 00000000
   00000000 00000000 00000000 00000000
114.   Offline scn: 0x0000.00000000 prev_range: 0
115.   Online Checkpointed at scn: 0x0000.00000000 01/01/88 00:00:00
116.   thread:0 rba:(0x0.0.0)
117.   enabled threads: 00000000 00000000 00000000 00000000
   00000000 00000000 00000000 00000000
118.   Hot Backup end marker scn: 0x0000.00000000
119.   DATA FILE #2:
120.   (name #5) /ifx/oradata1/oradata/ORA8DB/rbs01.dbf
121.   creation size=7680 block size=2048 status=0xe head=5 tail=5
   dup=1
```

Figure 6.6   Continued

```
122.   tablespace 1, index=2 krfil=2 prev_file=0
123.   unrecoverable scn: 0x0000.00000000 01/01/88 00:00:00
124.   Checkpoint cnt:422 scn: 0x0000.000047aa 01/16/99 08:38:45
125.   Stop scn: 0xffff.ffffffff 09/15/98 12:24:33
126.   Creation Checkpointed at scn: 0x0000.000021f6 01/16/98
       16:01:42
127.   thread:1 rba:(0x3a.2de.90)
128.   enabled threads: 01000000 00000000 00000000 00000000
       00000000 00000000 00000000 00000000
129.   Offline scn: 0x0000.00000000 prev_range: 0
130.   Online Checkpointed at scn: 0x0000.00000000 01/01/88 00:00:00
131.   thread:0 rba:(0x0.0.0)
132.   enabled threads: 00000000 00000000 00000000 00000000
       00000000 00000000 00000000 00000000
133.   Hot Backup end marker scn: 0x0000.00000000
134.   DATA FILE #3:
135.   (name #6) /ifx/oradata1/oradata/ORA8DB/temp01.dbf
136.   creation size=275 block size=2048 status=0xe head=6 tail=6
       dup=1
137.   tablespace 2, index=3 krfil=3 prev_file=0
138.   unrecoverable scn: 0x0000.00000000 01/01/88 00:00:00
139.   Checkpoint cnt:422 scn: 0x0000.000047aa 01/16/99 08:38:45
140.   Stop scn: 0xffff.ffffffff 09/15/98 12:24:33
141.   Creation Checkpointed at scn: 0x0000.000021fc 01/16/98
       16:01:43
142.   thread:1 rba:(0x3a.2e9.bc)
143.   enabled threads: 01000000 00000000 00000000 00000000
       00000000 00000000 00000000 00000000
144.   Offline scn: 0x0000.00000000 prev_range: 0
145.   Online Checkpointed at scn: 0x0000.00000000 01/01/88 00:00:00
146.   thread:0 rba:(0x0.0.0)
147.   enabled threads: 00000000 00000000 00000000 00000000
       00000000 00000000 00000000 00000000
148.   Hot Backup end marker scn: 0x0000.00000000
149.   DATA FILE #4:
150.   (name #7) /ifx/oradata1/oradata/ORA8DB/tools01.dbf
151.   creation size=12800 block size=2048 status=0xe head=7 tail=7
       dup=1
152.   tablespace 3, index=4 krfil=4 prev_file=0
153.   unrecoverable scn: 0x0000.00000000 01/01/88 00:00:00
154.   Checkpoint cnt:422 scn: 0x0000.000047aa 01/16/99 08:38:45
155.   Stop scn: 0xffff.ffffffff 09/15/98 12:24:33
```

Figure 6.6   Continued

```
156.   Creation Checkpointed at scn: 0x0000.00002202 01/16/98
       16:01:59
157.   thread:1 rba:(0x3a.2f4.c0)
158.   enabled threads: 01000000 00000000 00000000 00000000
       00000000 00000000 00000000 00000000
159.   Offline scn: 0x0000.00000000 prev_range: 0
160.   Online Checkpointed at scn: 0x0000.00000000 01/01/88 00:00:00
161.   thread:0 rba:(0x0.0.0)
162.   enabled threads: 00000000 00000000 00000000 00000000
       00000000 00000000 00000000 00000000
163.   Hot Backup end marker scn: 0x0000.00000000
164.   DATA FILE #5:
165.   (name #8) /ifx/oradata1/oradata/ORA8DB/users01.dbf
166.   creation size=512 block size=2048 status=0xe head=8 tail=8
       dup=1
167.   tablespace 4, index=5 krfil=5 prev_file=0
168.   unrecoverable scn: 0x0000.00000000 01/01/88 00:00:00
169.   Checkpoint cnt:422 scn: 0x0000.000047aa 01/16/99 08:38:45
170.   Stop scn: 0xffff.ffffffff 09/15/98 12:24:33
171.   Creation Checkpointed at scn: 0x0000.00002209 01/16/98
       16:02:01
172.   thread:1 rba:(0x3a.306.c0)
173.   enabled threads: 01000000 00000000 00000000 00000000
       00000000 00000000 00000000 00000000
174.   Offline scn: 0x0000.00000000 prev_range: 0
175.   Online Checkpointed at scn: 0x0000.00000000 01/01/88 00:00:00
176.   thread:0 rba:(0x0.0.0)
177.   enabled threads: 00000000 00000000 00000000 00000000
       00000000 00000000 00000000 00000000
178.   Hot Backup end marker scn: 0x0000.00000000
179.   TABLESPACE RECORDS:
180.   (blkno = 0x25, size = 68, max = 30, in-use = 5, last-recid=
       5)
181.   TABLESPACE #0 SYSTEM: recno=1
182.   First datafile link=1 Number of rollback segments=0
183.   Tablespace PITR mode start scn: 0x0000.00000000 01/01/88
       00:00:00
184.   Tablespace PITR last completion scn: 0x0000.00000000 01/01/88
       00:00:00
185.   TABLESPACE #1 RBS: recno=2
186.   First datafile link=2 Number of rollback segments=0
187.   Tablespace PITR mode start scn: 0x0000.00000000 01/01/88
       00:00:00
```

Figure 6.6   Continued

188. Tablespace PITR last completion scn: 0x0000.00000000 01/01/88
      00:00:00
189. TABLESPACE #2 TEMP: recno=3
190. First datafile link=3 Number of rollback segments=0
191. Tablespace PITR mode start scn: 0x0000.00000000 01/01/88
      00:00:00
192. Tablespace PITR last completion scn: 0x0000.00000000 01/01/88
      00:00:00
193. TABLESPACE #3 TOOLS: recno=4
194. First datafile link=4 Number of rollback segments=0
195. Tablespace PITR mode start scn: 0x0000.00000000 01/01/88
      00:00:00
196. Tablespace PITR last completion scn: 0x0000.00000000 01/01/88
      00:00:00
197. TABLESPACE #4 USERS: recno=5
198. First datafile link=5 Number of rollback segments=0
199. Tablespace PITR mode start scn: 0x0000.00000000 01/01/88
      00:00:00
200. Tablespace PITR last completion scn: 0x0000.00000000 01/01/88
      00:00:00
201. LOG FILE HISTORY RECORDS:
202. (blkno = 0x29, size = 36, max = 843, in-use = 467, last-
      recid= 467)
203. Earliest record:
204. RECID #1 Recno 1 Record timestamp 01/16/98 15:53:43 Thread=1
      Seq#=1 Link-Recid=0
205. Low scn: 0x0000.00000001 01/16/98 15:52:52 Next scn:
      0x0000.00000089
206. Latest record:
207. RECID #467 Recno 467 Record timestamp 01/16/98 16:35:07
      Thread=1 Seq#=467 Link-Recid=466
208. Low scn: 0x0000.000046e3 01/16/98 16:34:13 Next scn:
      0x0000.00004724
209. RECID #466 Recno 466 Record timestamp 01/16/98 16:34:13
      Thread=1 Seq#=466 Link-Recid=465
210. Low scn: 0x0000.000046d4 01/16/98 16:34:08 Next scn:
      0x0000.000046e3
211. RECID #465 Recno 465 Record timestamp 01/16/98 16:34:08
      Thread=1 Seq#=465 Link-Recid=464
212. Low scn: 0x0000.000046c7 01/16/98 16:34:04 Next scn:
      0x0000.000046d4
213. RECID #464 Recno 464 Record timestamp 01/16/98 16:34:04
      Thread=1 Seq#=464 Link-Recid=463

Figure 6.6   Continued

```
214.  Low scn: 0x0000.000046b9 01/16/98 16:33:59 Next scn:
      0x0000.000046c7
215.  RECID #463 Recno 463 Record timestamp 01/16/98 16:33:59
      Thread=1 Seq#=463 Link-Recid=462
216.  Low scn: 0x0000.000046a3 01/16/98 16:33:50 Next scn:
      0x0000.000046b9
217.  RECID #462 Recno 462 Record timestamp 01/16/98 16:33:50
      Thread=1 Seq#=462 Link-Recid=461
218.  Low scn: 0x0000.00004698 01/16/98 16:33:48 Next scn:
      0x0000.000046a3
219.  OFFLINE RANGE RECORDS:
220.  (blkno = 0x38, size = 56, max = 36, in-use = 0, last-recid=
      0)
221.  ARCHIVED LOG RECORDS:
222.  (blkno = 0x39, size = 584, max = 800, in-use = 0, last-recid=
      0)
223.  BACKUP SET RECORDS:
224.  (blkno = 0x120, size = 40, max = 50, in-use = 0, last-recid=
      0)
225.  BACKUP PIECE RECORDS:
226.  (blkno = 0x121, size = 736, max = 60, in-use = 0, last-recid=
      0)
227.  BACKUP DATAFILE RECORDS:
228.  (blkno = 0x137, size = 116, max = 69, in-use = 0, last-recid=
      0)
229.  BACKUP LOG RECORDS:
230.  (blkno = 0x13b, size = 76, max = 79, in-use = 0, last-recid=
      0)
231.  DATAFILE COPY RECORDS:
232.  (blkno = 0x13e, size = 660, max = 61, in-use = 0, last-recid=
      0)
233.  BACKUP DATAFILE CORRUPTION RECORDS:
234.  (blkno = 0x152, size = 44, max = 46, in-use = 0, last-recid=
      0)
235.  DATAFILE COPY CORRUPTION RECORDS:
236.  (blkno = 0x153, size = 40, max = 50, in-use = 0, last-recid=
      0)
237.  DELETION RECORDS:
238.  (blkno = 0x154, size = 20, max = 809, in-use = 0, last-recid=
      0)
239.  *** END OF DUMP ***
```

Figure 6.6   Continued

In addition to the information to be found in the Oracle7 control file the following sections are added in Oracle8:

- checkpoint progress records
- tablespace records
- offline range records
- archived log records
- backup set records
- backup piece records
- backup data file records
- backup log records
- data file copy records
- backup data file corruption records
- data file copy corruption records
- deletion records.

As can be seen from the above list, most of the changes to the control file have been made to support the Oracle Recovery Manager (RMAN) utility. Most of this information can be viewed by querying the appropriate V$ view as discussed earlier in this chapter.

Let's look at each of these new sections.

Checkpoint progress records (line 42)

Checkpoint progress records are used to record the state of the buffer cache in the SGA in case instance or crash recovery is required. In each record the *low cache rba* is an address within the redo log where recovery can begin. The *on disk rba* is the highest redo value that is on disk, and this value will be used during instance recovery to mark the point at which the re-application of redo should stop. The *on disk scn* is the SCN value corresponding to the *on disk rba* value. This SCN value is needed in case the *on disk rba* value points to a block that was never written. In this case instance recovery will stop at this SCN value.

Tablespace records (line 179)

This simply lists all of the tablespaces found in the database with a link to the first data file and gives an indication of the number of rollback segments the tablespace contains. It is included in the control file to record the start and completion SCN values for Tablespace Point-in-Time Recovery. A query of the V$TABLESPACE view also shows this information.

Offline range records (line 219)

Offline range records are created if a tablespace is either taken offline with the NORMAL parameter, is brought back online, is made read only or changed to read-write. Any tablespaces taken offline with the IMMEDIATE parameter do not get recorded. The information recorded is the SCN value at the time the tablespace is taken offline and the last SCN value at which is was checkpointed. This again controls the recovery process and application of redo for these tablespaces. It avoids Oracle applying redo unnecessarily during recovery for those tablespaces that were offline at the time of a crash (assuming these tablespaces were not affected).

Archived log records (line 221)

These records are written when an online redo log is archived. The thread number, log sequence number, and resetlogs change number are recorded for the file. If the archived log is restored from a backup with RMAN then an archived log record is also created. You can also use the V$ARCHIVED_LOGS view to see this information.

Backup set records, backup piece records, backup data file records (lines 223, 225, 227)

These records are written by RMAN when a backup completes successfully. For *Backup set records* the type of backup is recorded (archive logs, incremental or full data file) together with the number of backup pieces. Each *backup piece record* shows details of each backup piece in the set and the *backup data file records* show information about each data file included in the backup. All of these records have corresponding V$ views as discussed earlier.

Backup log records (line 229)

RMAN will write these types of records to the control file after having successfully backed up the archived redo logs.

Data file copy records (line 231)

These records are written by RMAN after a successful image backup of each data file using the RMAN COPY command

Backup data file corruption records, data file copy corruption records (lines 233, 235)

During backup, RMAN performs a sanity check on each data block before writing to the backup device. If it finds any corrupt blocks, it will write a corruption record showing the starting block where the corruption is found together with the number of blocks that are corrupted from that point. If RMAN is performing a data file image copy it will write a *data file copy corruption record*, otherwise it will write a *backup data file corruption record*.

Deletion records (lines 237)

Finally, deletion records are created to help RMAN perform a backup catalog RESYNC operation. A DBA can force RMAN to resync the catalog to update it with the latest backup or restore information. RMAN will use deletion records to determine what has been deleted from a backup. These records are created every time an archived redo log, data file copy or backup piece is deleted.

Understanding redo log dumps

The most useful part of the redo log is the file header. It is very rare that dumping the contents of the redo log will be of any use to the DBA. We will show you how to dump the contents of the redo log, in case you need to do this for Oracle technical support, but most of the information in the redo log itself is highly technical and not of much use in debugging everyday problems.

We described earlier in this chapter how to dump the redo log file header using the REDOHDR event. The information written to the trace file will be similar to Figure 6.7 and most of this information will be familiar to you by now as you will have seen it in the control file.

```
 1. Dump file
    /ora/app/oracle/admin/P6Q_ORA/udump/p6q_ora_ora_512.trc
 2. Oracle7 Server Release 7.3.2.1.0 - Production Release
 3. With the parallel query option
 4. PL/SQL Release 2.3.2.0.0 - Production
 5. ORACLE_HOME = /ora/app/oracle/product/7.3.2
 6. System name: SunOS
 7. Node name:   ptchp6q
 8. Release:   5.5.1
 9. Version:   Generic
10.Machine:   sun4m
11.Instance name: P6Q_ORA
12.Redo thread mounted by this instance: 1
13.Oracle process number: 7
14.Unix process pid: 512, image: oracleP6Q_ORA
15.Sat Jan 16 10:05:40 1999
16.*** SESSION ID:(5.60) 1999.01.16.10.05.40.000
```

Figure 6.7   Contents of an Oracle7 redo header dump

```
17.DUMP OF LOG FILES: 3 logs in database
18.LOG FILE #1:
19.(name #1) /ora/app/oracle/oradata/P6Q_ORA/redoP6Q_ORA01.log
20.Thread 1 redo log links: forward: 2 backward: 0
21.siz: 0x3e8 seq: 0x00000064 hws: 0x9 bsz: 512 nab: 0x3e6 flg: 0x0
   dup: 1
22.Archive links: fwrd: 0 back: 0 Prev scn: 0x0000.0000362d
23.Low scn: 0x0000.00003736 09/15/98 10:01:58
24.Next scn: 0x0000.00003794 09/22/98 06:13:48
25.FILE HEADER:
26.Software vsn=117489664=0x700c000, Compatibility
   Vsn=117489664=0x700c000
27.Db Id=754995808=0x2d005260, Db Name='P6Q_ORA'
28.Control Seq=405=0x195, Creation file size=0=0x0 Current file
   size=1000=0x3e8
29.File Number=1, Blksiz=512, File Type=2
30.descrip:"Thread 0001, Seq# 0000000100, SCN 0x000000003736-
   0x000000003794"
31.thread: 1 nab: 0x3e6 seq: 0x00000064 hws: 0x9 eot: 0 dis: 0
32.reset logs count: 0x0 scn: 0x0000.00000000
33.Low scn: 0x0000.00003736 09/15/98 10:01:58
34.Next scn: 0x0000.00003794 09/22/98 06:13:48
35.Enabled scn: 0x0000.00000001 01/12/98 18:51:14
36.Thread closed scn: 0x0000.00003740 09/15/98 12:24:13
37.Log format vsn: 0x7009000 Disk cksum: 0x0 Calc cksum: 0xd54c
38.LOG FILE #2:
39.(name #2) /ora/app/oracle/oradata/P6Q_ORA/redoP6Q_ORA02.log
40.Thread 1 redo log links: forward: 3 backward: 1
41.siz: 0x3e8 seq: 0x00000065 hws: 0x6 bsz: 512 nab: 0x3e9 flg: 0x0
   dup: 1
42.Archive links: fwrd: 0 back: 0 Prev scn: 0x0000.00003736
43.Low scn: 0x0000.00003794 09/22/98 06:13:48
44.Next scn: 0x0000.000037df 09/22/98 06:29:58
45.FILE HEADER:
46.Software vsn=117489664=0x700c000, Compatibility
   Vsn=117489664=0x700c000
47.Db Id=754995808=0x2d005260, Db Name='P6Q_ORA'
48.Control Seq=405=0x195, Creation file size=0=0x0 Current file
   size=1000=0x3e8
49.File Number=2, Blksiz=512, File Type=2
50.descrip:"Thread 0001, Seq# 0000000101, SCN 0x000000003794-
   0x0000000037df"
```

Figure 6.7   Continued

```
51.thread: 1 nab: 0x3e9 seq: 0x00000065 hws: 0x6 eot: 0 dis: 0
52.resct logs count: 0x0 scn: 0x0000.00000000
53.Low scn: 0x0000.00003794 09/22/98 06:13:48
54.Next scn: 0x0000.000037df 09/22/98 06:29:58
55.Enabled scn: 0x0000.00000001 01/12/98 18:51:14
56.Thread closed scn: 0x0000.00003794 09/22/98 06:13:48
57.Log format vsn: 0x7009000 Disk cksum: 0x0 Calc cksum: 0xfb06
58.LOG FILE #3:
59.(name #3) /ora/app/oracle/oradata/P6Q_ORA/redoP6Q_ORA03.log
60.Thread 1 redo log links: forward: 0 backward: 2
61.siz: 0x3e8 seq: 0x00000066 hws: 0xd bsz: 512 nab: 0xffffffff
   flg: 0x8 dup: 1
62.Archive links: fwrd: 0 back: 0 Prev scn: 0x0000.00003794
63.Low scn: 0x0000.000037df 09/22/98 06:29:58
64.Next scn: 0xffff.ffffffff 09/15/98 10:01:58
65.FILE HEADER:
66.Software vsn=117489664=0x700c000, Compatibility
   Vsn=117489664=0x700c000
67.Db Id=754995808=0x2d005260, Db Name='P6Q_ORA'
68.Control Seq=405=0x195, Creation file size=0=0x0 Current file
   size=1000=0x3e8
69.File Number=3, Blksiz=512, File Type=2
70.descrip:"Thread 0001, Seq# 0000000102, SCN 0x0000000037df-
   0xffffffffffffff"
71.thread: 1 nab: 0xffffffff seq: 0x00000066 hws: 0xd eot: 1 dis: 0
72.reset logs count: 0x0 scn: 0x0000.00000000
73.Low scn: 0x0000.000037df 09/22/98 06:29:58
74.Next scn: 0xffff.ffffffff 09/15/98 10:01:58
75.Enabled scn: 0x0000.00000001 01/12/98 18:51:14
76.Thread closed scn: 0x0000.000038e7 10/02/98 11:58:08
77.Log format vsn: 0x7009000 Disk cksum: 0x0 Calc cksum: 0xc156
```

Figure 6.7   Continued

In Oracle7, when dumping the log file header, the trace file will also contain the corresponding entries from the control file. Lines 18 to 24 in Figure 6.7 are from the control file. Line 25 is where the redo log file header begins. Lines 26 to 29 show the generic file header which details the Oracle software version, the oldest version of Oracle with which the format of the redo log is compatible, the internal database id and database name to which the redo log belongs, and information about the file size. Lines 30 to 36 are derived from the actual log file header and this information should be identical to lines 18 to 24 which were read from the control file.

Line 30 is perhaps the most important line for the DBA because it shows which thread each log group belongs to, the sequence number of the log, and the low and high SCN values for the log. If the high SCN value is set to infinity then that indicates that it is the current log being written to by the Oracle background process LGWR.

In Oracle8 an extra line appears showing the *disk checksum* and the *calculated checksum*. Any differences between these two indicates possible corruption in the redo log.

Dumping redo entries

As stated earlier, you will only need to dump the actual contents of the redo log if required by Oracle technical support, the information it contains is not of direct use to the DBA. If you need to dump redo entries then use the ALTER SYSTEM DUMP LOGFILE command within Server Manager. This command allows you:

- to dump the entire contents of both the online and archived redo log file;

- a range of redo entries defined either by an rba address range (which is the address of the redo log information of interest), a data block address range, or a time range;

- a type of redo entry such as commit records.

Understanding data file dumps

The data file header is more useful to the DBA investigating possible recovery scenarios than the actual contents of the data file itself. If the contents of a data file need to be dumped it is because of a specific block corruption problem and Oracle technical support need to see the contents of the block.

Here we will only discuss the data file header dumps. To dump the contents of a data file you need to use the BLOCKDUMP event, to dump the data file headers use the FILE_HDRS event. Both of these events were discussed earlier. The format of the file headers changed between Oracle7 and Oracle8 so we discuss them separately.

Oracle7 data file header

Figure 6.8 shows the contents of a data file header dump.

```
1. Dump file
   /ora/app/oracle/admin/P6Q_ORA/udump/p6q_ora_ora_539.trc
2. Oracle7 Server Release 7.3.2.1.0 - Production Release
3. With the parallel query option
4. PL/SQL Release 2.3.2.0.0 - Production
5. ORACLE_HOME = /ora/app/oracle/product/7.3.2
```

Figure 6.8   Partial contents of an Oracle7 data file header dump

```
 6. System name: SunOS
 7. Node name:    ptchp6q
 8. Release:   5.5.1
 9. Version:   Generic
10.Machine:   sun4m
11.Instance name: P6Q_ORA
12.Redo thread mounted by this instance: 1
13.Oracle process number: 7
14.Unix process pid: 539, image: oracleP6Q_ORA
15.Sat Jan 16 11:01:16 1999
16.*** SESSION ID:(5.87) 1999.01.16.11.01.16.000
17.DUMP OF DATA FILES: 9 files in database
18.DATA FILE #1:
19.(name #4) /ora/app/oracle/oradata/P6Q_ORA/system01.dbf
20.creation size=20480 block size=2048 status=0xf head=4 tail=4
   dup=1
21.Checkpoint cnt:144 scn: 0x0000.000038e8 stop scn:
   0xffff.ffffffff 10/02/98 11:58:08
22.Creation Checkpointed at scn: 0x0000.00000003 01/12/98 18:51:29
23.thread:1 rba:(0x1.3.10)
24.enabled threads: 01000000 00000000 00000000 00000000 00000000
   00000000 00000000 00000000
25.Offline scn: 0x0000.00000000
26.Online Checkpointed at scn: 0x0000.00000000 01/01/88 00:00:00
27.thread:0 rba:(0x0.0.0)
28.enabled threads: 00000000 00000000 00000000 00000000 00000000
   00000000 00000000 00000000
29.Hot Backup end marker scn: 0x0000.00000000
30.FILE HEADER:
31.Software vsn=117489664=0x700c000, Compatibility
   Vsn=117485568=0x700b000
32.Db Id=754995808=0x2d005260, Db Name='P6Q_ORA'
33.Control Seq=405=0x195, Creation file size=0=0x0 Current file
   size=20480=0x5000
34.File Number=1, Blksiz=2048, File Type=3
35.Creation at scn: 0x0000.00000003 01/12/98 18:51:29
36.Backup taken at scn: 0x0000.00000000 01/01/88 00:00:00 thread:0
37.reset logs count:0x0 scn: 0x0000.00000000 recovered at 01/01/88
   00:00:00
38.status:0x104 root dba:0x04000179 chkpt cnt: 144 ctl cnt:143
39.begin-hot-backup file size: 0
```

Figure 6.8   Continued

```
40.Checkpointed at scn: 0x0000.000038e8 01/16/99 08:38:06
41.thread:1 rba:(0x66.3c9.10)
42.enabled threads: 01000000 00000000 00000000 00000000 00000000
   00000000 00000000 00000000
43.Backup Checkpointed at scn: 0x0000.00000000 01/01/88 00:00:00
44.thread:0 rba:(0x0.0.0)
45.enabled threads: 00000000 00000000 00000000 00000000 00000000
   00000000 00000000 00000000
46.DATA FILE #2:
```

Figure 6.8   Continued

The trace also writes the information found in the control file for the data file and in
our example this is shown at lines 18 to 29. The information shown between lines 35 and
45 is taken from the actual data file header. The *Checkpointed at scn* in the actual file header
shown, at line 40, should be the same as the SCN found in the control file (line 21).
Similarly the *chkpt cnt* value on line 38 should match that found on line 21 (*Checkpoint cnt*).
If these values are different it indicates that an old data file has been restored and that is
how Oracle knows the file requires media recovery.

Oracle8 data file header

Figure 6.9 shows a data file header dump taken from an Oracle8 database.

```
 1. Dump file /oracle/app/admin/ORA8DB/udump/ora8db_ora_562.trc
 2. Oracle8 Enterprise Edition Release 8.0.3.0.0 - Production
 3. With the Partitioning and Objects options
 4. PL/SQL Release 8.0.3.0.0 - Production
 5. ORACLE_HOME = /oracle/app/product/8.0.3
 6. System name: SunOS
 7. Node name:   ptchp6q
 8. Release:   5.5.1
 9. Version:   Generic
10.Machine:   sun4m
11.Instance name: ORA8DB
12.Redo thread mounted by this instance: 1
13.Oracle process number: 8
14.Unix process pid: 562, image: oracleORA8DB
15.Sat Jan 16 11:12:28 1999
```

Figure 6.9   Partial contents of an Oracle8 data file header dump

```
16.*** SESSION ID:(9.44) 1999.01.16.11.12.28.000
17.DUMP OF DATA FILES: 5 files in database
18.DATA FILE #1:
19.(name #4) /ifx/oradata1/oradata/ORA8DB/system01.dbf
20.creation size=40960 block size=2048 status=0xe head=4 tail=4
   dup=1
21.tablespace 0, index=1 krfil=1 prev_file=0
22.unrecoverable scn: 0x0000.00000000 01/01/88 00:00:00
23.Checkpoint cnt:480 scn: 0x0000.000047aa 01/16/99 08:38:45
24.Stop scn: 0xffff.ffffffff 09/15/98 12:24:33
25.Creation Checkpointed at scn: 0x0000.00000003 01/16/98 15:53:37
26.thread:1 rba:(0x1.3.10)
27.enabled threads: 01000000 00000000 00000000 00000000 00000000
   00000000 00000000 00000000
28.Offline scn: 0x0000.00000000 prev_range: 0
29.Online Checkpointed at scn: 0x0000.00000000 01/01/88 00:00:00
30.thread:0 rba:(0x0.0.0)
31.enabled threads: 00000000 00000000 00000000 00000000 00000000
   00000000 00000000 00000000
32.Hot Backup end marker scn: 0x0000.00000000
33.FILE HEADER:
34.Software vsn=134217728=0x8000000, Compatibility
   Vsn=134217728=0x8000000
35.Db Id=2887985999=0xac232b4f, Db Name='ORA8DB'
36.Control Seq=1448=0x5a8, File size=40960=0xa000
37.File Number=1, Blksiz=2048, File Type=3
38.Tablespace #0 - SYSTEM rel_fn:1
39.Creation at scn: 0x0000.00000003 01/16/98 15:53:37
40.Backup taken at scn: 0x0000.00000000 01/01/88 00:00:00 thread:0
41.reset logs count:0x133cf1cf scn: 0x0000.00000001 recovered at
   01/01/88 00:00:00
42.status:0x4 root dba:0x0040020f chkpt cnt: 480 ctl cnt:479
43.begin-hot-backup file size: 0
44.Checkpointed at scn: 0x0000.000047aa 01/16/99 08:38:45
45.thread:1 rba:(0x1d4.305.10)
46.enabled threads: 01000000 00000000 00000000 00000000 00000000
   00000000 00000000 00000000
47.Backup Checkpointed at scn: 0x0000.00000000 01/01/88 00:00:00
48.thread:0 rba:(0x0.0.0)
49.enabled threads: 00000000 00000000 00000000 00000000 00000000
   00000000 00000000 00000000
50.External cache id: 0x0 0x0 0x0 0x0
51.Absolute fuzzy scn: 0x0000.00000000
```

Figure 6.9   Continued

```
52.Recovery fuzzy scn: 0x0000.00000000 01/01/88 00:00:00
53.DATA FILE #2:
54.(name #5) /ifx/oradata1/oradata/ORA8DB/rbs01.dbf
55.creation size=7680 block size=2048 status=0xe head=5 tail=5
   dup=1
56.tablespace 1, index=2 krfil=2 prev_file=0
57.unrecoverable scn: 0x0000.00000000 01/01/88 00:00:00
58.Checkpoint cnt:422 scn: 0x0000.000047aa 01/16/99 08:38:45
59.Stop scn: 0xffff.ffffffff 09/15/98 12:24:33
60.Creation Checkpointed at scn: 0x0000.000021f6 01/16/98 16:01:42
61.thread:1 rba:(0x3a.2de.90)
62.enabled threads: 01000000 00000000 00000000 00000000 00000000
   00000000 00000000 00000000
63.Offline scn: 0x0000.00000000 prev_range: 0
64.Online Checkpointed at scn: 0x0000.00000000 01/01/88 00:00:00
65.thread:0 rba:(0x0.0.0)
66.enabled threads: 00000000 00000000 00000000 00000000 00000000
   00000000 00000000 00000000
67.Hot Backup end marker scn: 0x0000.00000000
68.FILE HEADER:
69.Software vsn=134217728=0x8000000, Compatibility
   Vsn=134217728=0x8000000
70.Db Id=2887985999=0xac232b4f, Db Name='ORA8DB'
71.Control Seq=1448=0x5a8, File size=7680=0x1e00
72.File Number=2, Blksiz=2048, File Type=3
73.Tablespace #1 - RBS rel_fn:2
74.Creation at scn: 0x0000.000021f6 01/16/98 16:01:42
75.Backup taken at scn: 0x0000.00000000 01/01/88 00:00:00 thread:0
76.reset logs count:0x133cf1cf scn: 0x0000.00000001 recovered at
   01/01/88 00:00:00
77.status:0x4 root dba:0x00000000 chkpt cnt: 422 ctl cnt:421
78.begin-hot-backup file size: 0
79.Checkpointed at scn: 0x0000.000047aa 01/16/99 08:38:45
80.thread:1 rba:(0x1d4.305.10)
81.enabled threads: 01000000 00000000 00000000 00000000 00000000
   00000000 00000000 00000000
82.Backup Checkpointed at scn: 0x0000.00000000 01/01/88 00:00:00
83.thread:0 rba:(0x0.0.0)
84.enabled threads: 00000000 00000000 00000000 00000000 00000000
   00000000 00000000 00000000
85.External cache id: 0x0 0x0 0x0 0x0
86.Absolute fuzzy scn: 0x0000.00000000
87.Recovery fuzzy scn: 0x0000.00000000 01/01/88 00:00:00
```

Figure 6.9   Continued

Line 22 shows the *unrecoverable scn value*, taken from the control file, which is updated when an unrecoverable write (or direct write, bypassing the buffer cache) is successfully made to the data file. This can be useful to the DBA who can now compare this value to the SCN value found in the backup of this data file. If the value in the backup data file is lower, the data file cannot be used for recovery and therefore should be deleted.

Line 38 shows basic information about the data file including the tablespace number to which this data file belongs and the relative file number of the data file. Line 43 shows the size of the data file at the start of a hot backup (updated by the `ALTER TABLESPACE BEGIN BACKUP` command) and this is recorded to avoid file checks failing if the file is extended in the middle of a hot backup. A non-zero value indicates that the tablespace is currently in hot backup mode. Line 47 shows the *Backup Checkpointed at scn* value which is incremented every time a checkpoint takes place whilst the tablespace is in hot backup mode. This is used because the *Checkpointed at scn* value is frozen when the tablespace is in hot backup mode. Should the tablespace be taken offline with the `IMMEDIATE` option, or the database crashes, the *Backup Checkpointed at scn* can be copied to the *Checkpointed at scn*. When using RMAN for hot backups you do not need to put the tablespace in hot backup mode.

6.2.5   Oracle internal recovery mechanisms

Redo log records

It is important to understand why Oracle generates redo, when this occurs and how Oracle uses redo in order to recover.

A redo record, as written to the online log files, consists of several records known as *change vectors*. Each change vector describes a single change made to a single block in the database. The block can be a data block belonging to a table, an index block or a rollback segment block. Each record contains a version number, the operation code of the transaction that generated the change, and the block address that the change belongs to. When the change vector is first built, the version number of the changed block is copied to the vector record. During recovery Oracle will apply the change to the changed block and update the block version number by one.

A redo record contains a group of change vectors that describe a single atomic change to the database. During recovery Oracle will either apply all change vectors for a redo record, or none at all, to ensure that the atomic nature of the change is maintained.

To make this clearer let's take an example. Consider the following SQL statement:

```
SQL> update dept set deptno=607 where deptno = 605;
```

We will assume that there is an index on the **dept** table containing the **deptno** column.
    The redo record would be constructed as follows:

- The update will first have to write an undo entry to the transaction table of the rollback segment. The transaction table entry will contain the address of the changed block, the status of the transaction (either active or commit), which in this case will be active, and the location within the rollback segment where the undo record for this update can be found. Since the transaction table is another block in the database that is being changed, a change vector is generated which contains the change for the transaction table block.

- The next step is to store the old `deptno` value of 605, in the rollback segment itself. Again this is a change to a block in the database so the next change vector contains the change to the rollback segment.

- The next change vector contains the change to the data block for the `dept` table.

- We also have an index on the `dept` table which will cause an index block to be changed (we are updating an indexed column). This will generate another redo record because another database object is affected. This redo record will also contain several change vectors for the rollback segment transaction table, change to the rollback segment block, and the index update.

- When a commit is executed yet a third redo record will be created for this.

Oracle's level of recovery is the transaction, so if we need to recover this update Oracle will either apply all three redo records, or none of them, to maintain transaction integrity.

Oracle7 introduced some optimization of redo that is generated. If more space is available in the rollback segment, Oracle will use it and avoid changing the transaction table again, therefore fewer change vectors are created.

The System Change Number (SCN)

Throughout our discussion of the contents of the redo logs, control files and data files we kept referring to the System Change Number (SCN). This number is used by Oracle to determine which redo records to apply to which data files. In this section we discuss how this works and why the SCN is so important.

The basic definition of an SCN is a number that defines the committed state of a database at any point in time. When a transaction is committed, Oracle generates an SCN that is unique for that transaction, in fact that SCN will be unique to the database. For transactions that perform updates across distributed databases Oracle will take the highest SCN number and apply that to the transaction so there is never any problem with read consistency. This means that in a single database the SCN numbers may not be assigned sequentially and in all probability will skip several numbers.

In an OPS (Oracle Parallel Server) configuration, where multiple Oracle instances are accessing one database, Oracle generates a global SCN value that it then copies to a local SCN for the instance performing a commit. This guarantees that each SCN will be unique across all instances.

The SCN value never gets reset to zero unless the database is recreated. The precision of the SCN number is such that you will never run out of numbers. Even if you executed 16,000 transactions a second every day, it would take 500 years before you ran out of numbers.

Oracle's recovery is purely based on SCNs.

In our earlier discussion of the contents of various Oracle files, we mentioned several parameters that define various SCN values at different times. We will now look at these parameters and the role they play in recovery.

Low and high SCN

The low SCN and high SCN values define which transactions are contained in each redo log. When a log switch occurs, Oracle will set the high SCN value of the log file being closed to the highest SCN stored in the file. The next log file to be opened will have its low SCN set to the high SCN value + 1 of the previous log and its high SCN will be set to infinity.

Offline normal SCN

The offline normal SCN is stored in the data dictionary table TS$ when a tablespace is taken offline with the NORMAL option. The action of taking a tablespace offline causes a checkpoint that in turn generates the offline normal SCN value (amongst other things). Oracle uses this value when a tablespace is brought back online and is particularly useful when the database is opened using the RESETLOGS option (see the discussion of RESETLOGS later in this chapter).

   If the tablespace is taken offline using either the TEMPORARY or IMMEDIATE options the offline normal SCN will be set to zero. The impact this has is that the tablespace will not be able to be brought back online after using RESETLOGS.

Stop SCN

The stop SCN is used by Oracle to determine when to stop recovering data for a particular data file. The value is recorded in the control file (see our discussion of control files earlier) for every data file in a tablespace and is normally set to infinity. When the tablespace is taken offline, the stop SCN will be updated for every data file to the SCN value of the last transaction on that tablespace. No redo will be generated for the tablespace after the stop SCN is set.

Redo threads

As discussed in Chapter 3, the default R/3 installation creates two redo log groups, /oracle/<SID>/origlogA and /oracle/<SID>/origlogB which are also mirrored. A redo log group can contain one or more online redo log files that are identical and stored on separate disk devices. A collection of online redo log files is referred to as a *thread of redo*. In a single instance architecture, Oracle will create the redo log thread and give it a number of 1. It is possible to create additional threads for a single instance but Oracle will only use one of these threads. Each thread will point to a particular redo log group or groups and hence a particular set of redo log files.

   In the Oracle Parallel Server architecture, each instance will have its own redo thread uniquely identified with each thread pointing to the redo log group(s) specific to that instance. In order for Oracle to determine which set of redo records need to be applied from which thread, the thread number is stored in the control files and redo log files.

Redo log switches

A redo log switch occurs when either the current online redo log is full, or the DBA executes the `ALTER SYSTEM SWITCH LOGFILE` command. The log switch causes the `LGWR` process to close the current online redo log file and open the next available log file. The steps for performing a log switch are as follows:

- *Select log file to switch to* – to determine which log file to use, Oracle scans the control file for thread information and reads the list of files that are available for the current thread. Whilst scanning the control file, Oracle looks at the checkpoint information, archiving status of the log files and the availability of each file. If several log files are available for use, Oracle will open the one with the lowest sequence number. Once the log file is selected, Oracle will update the control file, alert log, previous online log, and newly selected log with various status flags. This includes setting the high SCN value for the previous online log and also the low SCN value for the new online log, as described earlier. These changes are made in such a way that if the process crashes whilst switching logs, Oracle recovery will recognize that the switch was not completed successfully.

- *Flush the redo log buffer in the SGA and disable redo generation* – in the SGA, Oracle maintains a status flag to indicate whether foreground processes are allowed to generate redo. During a log switch, redo generation is temporarily disabled. The redo log buffer stored in the SGA is then flushed to the current online redo log. During this procedure, any foreground processes that have already been allocated space in the redo log buffer (in other words they have already acquired a redo latch) will be allowed to continue to generate redo.

- *Update the control file and data file headers, close the log* – the control file is updated with the relevant log file information, the thread record is also updated and eventually the redo log file is closed. A new SCN is generated which uniquely identifies the log switch process. The `ARCH` background process will now start to archive the redo log to the archive directory.

- *Open newly selected log file* – the final step is to open the new log file group and make it the current log. If the redo log group has more than one file member, `LGWR` will attempt to open all files in the group. If there is a write error on any of the files in the group, `LGWR` will update the status of the file as STALE and will subsequently not attempt to write to it. For those file members it can write to it will mark them as OPEN and update the SCN which indicates that the log switch is complete.

When running Oracle Parallel Server (OPS), each thread performs log switches independently. This could potentially cause a problem due to the fact that the range of SCN values may vary considerably. Consider the situation where you are running R/3 in a two instance OPS configuration. Instance ABC is very active and instance DEF is not. The log file for instance ABC may have a *high SCN* value of 3,000,000 whereas instance DEF has a *high SCN* value of only 500. Should you lose the current online redo log file of instance DEF you would need to perform media recovery to a backup of your database. However the recovery would only be performed as far as SCN value 500 which means the changes between SCN 501 to 3,000,000 would be lost!

To avoid this situation, Oracle forces log switches to occur in all threads when the SCN range between threads gets too wide. So in our example, instance DEF would be forced to perform a log switch that would ensure it kept up with the SCN values. It is important to note **that you may still lose data but the amount lost would be smaller**. For this reason it is *very* important that you mirror your online redo logs to avoid this happening.

Checkpoints

A checkpoint is a database event that flushes modified data from the buffers in the SGA to disk. This may include data for both committed and uncommitted transactions. Once a checkpoint has been completed successfully, the redo for those changes is no longer required because all of the relevant data files have been updated on disk. Checkpoints are needed because of the circular nature of the redo logs. Before a redo log can be reused Oracle needs to make sure it has been archived successfully and that all changes for that log are on disk. Also, because data buffers are flushed to disk based on an LRU (Least Recently Used) algorithm, those buffers that are being constantly changed may never get flushed to disk. A checkpoint ensures that this happens regularly so that instance recovery is faster.

Several events trigger checkpoints:

- A checkpoint automatically starts at every log switch. If a previous checkpoint is currently active, a checkpoint forced by a log switch overrides it.

- The initialization parameter `LOG_CHECKPOINT_INTERVAL` will force a checkpoint when the number of redo log blocks indicated by this parameter have been written to disk since the last checkpoint.

- The `LOG_CHECKPOINT_TIMEOUT` parameter will force a checkpoint after a specific number of seconds have elapsed since the last checkpoint. Both this parameter, and the previous one, should be used if you have very large log files and your log switches are infrequent. Checkpoints triggered by these initialization parameters are not performed until the previous checkpoint has completed.

- The `ALTER TABLESPACE BEGIN BACKUP` command forces a checkpoint on all the data files that are part of the tablespace being backed up. A checkpoint at this time overrides any previous checkpoint still in progress.

- If the DBA takes a tablespace offline with the `NORMAL` or `TEMPORARY` parameters, a checkpoint is forced only on the online data files of the associated tablespace.

- When the DBA shuts down the database with either the `NORMAL` or `IMMEDIATE` parameters, Oracle forces a database checkpoint to complete before the instance is shut down. A checkpoint forced by instance shutdown overrides any previously running checkpoint.

- The DBA forces a checkpoint manually by executing the `ALTER SYSTEM CHECKPOINT` command. A checkpoint forced on demand overrides any previously running checkpoint.

There are three types of checkpoint that can be performed:

- **Local checkpoint** – where a checkpoint occurs for all data files on a single instance. The DBA can force this type of checkpoint to occur on the instance to which he/she is connected by executing the `ALTER SYSTEM CHECKPOINT LOCAL` command from the line mode Server Manager.

- **Global checkpoint** – this type of checkpoint occurs for all data files and all instances in an OPS environment. The command to force this type of checkpoint is `ALTER SYSTEM CHECKPOINT GLOBAL`. An SQL statement may also cause this type of checkpoint to occur, or when Oracle triggers a database-wide checkpoint automatically.

- **File checkpoint** – this causes a checkpoint to occur on a subset of data files for a specific database. In an OPS environment all instances will perform this checkpoint. The `ALTER TABLESPACE BEGIN BACKUP` command will force this type of checkpoint. A file checkpoint is always performed as a result of an SQL statement. Taking a tablespace offline also causes a file checkpoint.

The DBA must be aware that checkpoints can be I/O and CPU intensive depending on the amount of work the checkpoint has to perform, so make sure the checkpoint frequency is tuned carefully to avoid too much of a performance impact on the R/3 system.

Checkpoint processing

The work done during the checkpoint is largely the same irrespective of how the checkpoint is triggered. The only real difference is the process that performs the checkpoint. If the checkpoint is triggered by a command such as `ALTER TABLESPACE BEGIN BACKUP`, then the foreground process will execute the checkpoint. In all other situations, the checkpoint will be performed by either the `CKPT` background process or by the `LGWR` background process. In Oracle7 the `CKPT` process is manually enabled by setting `CHECK-POINT_PROCESS = TRUE` in the Oracle initialization file. If this is not done then the `LGWR` process will perform all checkpoints. You only need to set this parameter if the performance of LGWR degrades noticeably during a checkpoint. In Oracle8 the `CKPT` process is started automatically.

In order to process a *global checkpoint*, Oracle performs the following steps:

1. *Acquire an instance state enqueue* – Oracle requires this to ensure that the database will be kept open during the duration of a checkpoint. This enqueue prevents any instance from allowing the database to be shut down.

2. *Capture current checkpoint information* – Oracle will create a record in the SGA to record the current checkpoint time, the active threads, the current thread performing the checkpoint, and the address in the redo log file that will be the cutoff point for recovery.

3. *Identify dirty buffers* – Oracle scans each buffer cache in the SGA looking for the dirty buffers. For each buffer it comes across that affects the range of files to be checkpointed, Oracle marks the buffer as one to be flushed. Temporary segment buffers or read-only buffers are skipped during this process. Once all buffers are identified and marked, the DBWR process is woken up to perform the writes to disk.

4. *Flush the dirty buffers to disk* – DBWR is responsible for performing this step. When it completes it sets a flag to indicate it has finished. The checkpoint process will keep checking for this flag until it is set.

5. *Update data files and control files* – finally the control file and data file headers are updated with the information captured in step 2. As we discussed earlier, the control file will contain one checkpoint record for each enabled thread. Each data file header also contains a checkpoint record as well. There are two cases when the data file headers may not be updated. The first case is when the data file is in hot backup mode because the backup must contain the checkpoint SCN of when the backup started. The second case is if the checkpoint SCN is lower than the number in the data file header. This can happen if an ALTER TABLESPACE BEGIN BACKUP command is executed which affects the data file that is part of the checkpoint. The command may complete its checkpoint earlier.

Before writing to the data file headers, Oracle will verify them for consistency. Any files that fail this verification are ignored, and therefore their headers are not updated. Such a file would need media recovery if the online redo log, containing the changes for that file, is overwritten. In this case, DBWR will take the file offline. A counter of checkpoints is maintained in both the data file headers, and in the control file. This counter is used by Oracle to ensure the DBA does not restore the wrong version of a data file during recovery. It is also used at database startup to verify all data files are still current. If this check fails, the DBA receives an error on startup.

In Oracle8, the checkpoint algorithm has been modified. The dirty buffers in the SGA are now linked on a separate queue known as the *checkpoint queue*. Each buffer has a redo value associated with it, therefore the queue contains links to dirty buffers in ascending order of their redo value. The position of the buffer will not change even if it is modified more than once before it is written out to disk.

When a checkpoint occurs, Oracle will write out the buffers in the same order as they are in the queue. The checkpoint request passes a redo value to the DBWR process that will cause it to stop writing redo buffers to disk once the redo value of the buffer to be written is either equal to or greater than the checkpoint value. At this point the checkpoint is considered to be complete and the control file and data file headers are updated. This change means that multiple checkpoint requests can now be active and provides the following improvements over the Oracle7 checkpoint algorithm:

- DBWR always knows exactly which buffers need writing to satisfy a checkpoint request;

- every checkpoint write makes progress towards completing the earliest checkpoint;

- multiple checkpoint requests can be distinguished by their checkpoint redo values, therefore DBWR can complete them in order.

6.3   Oracle recovery methods

This section focuses on the recovery methods used by Oracle together with the various options the DBA has, at the database level, for recovery. Later in this chapter we will look at the options available when using SAP tools to perform recovery.

6.3.1   Applying redo log information

There are three basic types of recovery: online block recovery, thread recovery and media recovery. In all cases the application of redo log information is the same. Before we look at how this works, we need to understand the concepts of redo application, roll forward and rollback mechanisms that Oracle uses, and how Oracle decides when a data file(s) need recovery.

When a database is started Oracle performs the following steps:

1. Oracle reads the initialization file, determines the size of the SGA, creates it, and then starts the background processes. Assuming all of this goes alright, the instance is considered started and the database is in a *nomount* state.

2. Next the database is put into a *mount* state. This means that the control file is opened and the database mounted message is displayed. At this point it is possible to perform several commands such as ALTER DATABASE, RECOVER DATABASE and dump trace information using the ALTER SESSION command. Remember that at this stage the database is not open.

3. The final stage is to open the database ready for use. All the data file and log file headers are verified and each file opened. If the database is being opened for the first time after a database crash, Oracle will perform crash recovery automatically at this point, i.e. Oracle will firstly *roll forward* using the information in the online redo log files, then Oracle will perform a *rollback* of all transactions that had not been committed at the time of the crash. It takes the rollback information from the transaction tables of the rollback segments in the database.

One of the most frequently asked questions is how does Oracle know when crash recovery is required?

From our earlier discussions we know that Oracle stores a checkpoint counter in every data file header and that this information is also written to the control file. Oracle also maintains a *start SCN* in every data file header and the control file has a *stop SCN* specified for every data file. During normal operation of the database, the *start SCN* in the data file is incremented every time a checkpoint occurs and the *stop SCN* in the control file is set to infinity.

When the database is shut down with the NORMAL or IMMEDIATE parameters, a checkpoint is issued which causes the *stop SCN* in the control file to be set to the same value as the *start SCN* in the data file header. This happens for every data file. The next time the database is started, Oracle will firstly check that the checkpoint counter for each data file is the same as the checkpoint counter recorded in the control file. If any data file fails this check, which it will if the DBA has restored any data file from a backup (in this case the file header will have a different checkpoint counter value), Oracle will ask the DBA to apply media recovery. From the data file header Oracle knows which archived redo log file contains the redo data and prompts the DBA to supply the location of this file. If this first check succeeds then Oracle will check the *start SCN* value in the data file header with the corresponding *stop SCN* value in the control file. If they match, the data file is opened and the *stop SCN* is again set to infinity, if not then Oracle detects that thread recovery needs to be performed which it starts automatically, as described in step 3 above.

The roll forward process

Rolling forward requires Oracle to sequentially apply all the redo log records to the corresponding data blocks in the data file(s) being recovered. To do this, Oracle first opens the log file for each thread that was enabled at the time the SCN was allocated. If the log file is online then it is automatically opened. If an archived log is required, then the DBA is prompted to enter its location, and the sequence number is supplied from the data file header. The redo is applied in the same order as it was generated. If recovery is performed in the OPS environment, then Oracle may switch threads during recovery.

Every data block has a version number and each change vector for the block also has a version number. When a data file is restored, the version numbers of all of the blocks will be lower than those in the corresponding vector records, therefore Oracle will apply redo records in order of the version number for each block. Figure 6.10 shows an example of rolling a data block forward from an online redo log file.

In Figure 6.10 the block in the data file has a version number of 5. From the redo log Oracle will apply the change vector record containing the change to the block that has a version number of 6, then it will apply the next change vector record taking the block to version 7 and so on until all changes have been applied in sequence.

It can happen that the data block version number is actually ahead of the change vector version number. This will happen if a single data file is restored from a backup and all the other data files are current. Oracle will still read each change vector in turn, if it finds the data block version is ahead of the one it finds in the redo log it will skip and go to the next. So even though recovery will only be applied to the one data file, in our example, the redo for the other data files will still be examined. Oracle does not have to examine each data block, it simply checks the *redo SCN* against the *checkpoint SCN* in the data file header.

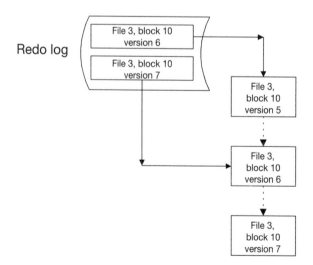

Figure 6.10   Rolling a data block forward

Rolling back

Once Oracle has completed the roll forward it then performs the rollback process. To do this it has to access the rollback segments in the database. These are recovered during the roll forward, hence the reason why Oracle performs a roll forward first!

Oracle finds the rollback segment transaction tables by querying the data dictionary object UNDO$. It scans the transaction tables for transactions marked as ACTIVE, in other words these are transactions that had not yet been committed prior to the failure. It is not unusual for Oracle to generate large amounts of redo that causes redo log archiving to occur. Because the roll back is changing the data blocks, redo change vector records will be created. At this point the recovery will be complete.

One rollback segment requires special mention, the SYSTEM rollback segment. Undo generated by changes to the data dictionary table UNDO$ is recorded in this rollback segment. If this segment becomes corrupted, Oracle will not be able to rebuild the UNDO$ table and therefore will not be able to find the transaction tables in order to rollback uncommitted transactions. The SYSTEM rollback segment should therefore be backed up securely.

6.3.2 Block level recovery

Block level recovery is automatically performed by Oracle and does not involve any action from the DBA. It is included here so that the DBA understands when this type of recovery occurs and will know what Oracle has attempted to do should Oracle be unable to recover a block and therefore signals an error that the DBA will have to resolve.

When Oracle detects a corrupted block in the buffer cache, it tries to read it from disk and recover it using information from the online redo logs. It uses the online redo log containing change vectors for changes that have not yet been checkpointed against the block. Recovery stops at the end of the redo log with the version number of the change vector that was current at the time block recovery started. If an error occurs during recovery, Oracle will mark the block as corrupt and issue an error message. The DBA should then arrange to dump the block using the BLOCKDUMP event as described earlier. Sometimes the PMON background process will perform block level recovery, but the amount of time it spends recovering is limited. The number of redo blocks it applies is hardcoded into the PMON process and varies by operating system. This number is not configurable.

6.3.3 Terminated threads

When considering thread recovery we have to distinguish between a single-instance Oracle database and the Oracle Parallel Server (OPS) where multiple instances are accessing one database. In a single-instance database, thread recovery is performed as part of crash recovery when the crashed database is re-opened. The process Oracle uses is the same as described here, but it is much simpler because only one thread is involved. Our discussion of terminated threads, therefore, will discuss how Oracle recovers when more than one thread is involved, as in an OPS configuration.

In an OPS environment, terminated threads can be recovered as part of either instance recovery or crash recovery. Instance recovery is performed when one of the instances dies and another instance detects this. This instance will then recover the terminated thread for the dead instance. It will also clear any locks held by that instance after thread recovery has completed. If the DBA restarts the dead instance before instance recovery is completed, then Oracle will recover the thread during crash recovery as it does in a single-instance configuration. If all instances fail at the same time, the first instance to be restarted will perform the crash recovery.

Thread recovery involves applying all redo changes as part of the thread that have occurred since the last thread checkpoint. If the thread was in the middle of a redo log switch at the time of failure, thread recovery rolls back the changes and calculates the next available block to which redo can be written in the redo log file. It also calculates the highest SCN to be used by the dead instance.

If an instance attempts to open a database whilst crash recovery is being performed, the instance will wait until recovery has completed successfully. The redo for each thread can be applied independently because only one cache can have changes for a given block at any point in time. Therefore to recover a specific thread, only that thread's redo logs are required. If multiple threads need recovery however, Oracle will recover them one at a time.

6.3.4   Recovering from media failure

Whilst block and thread recovery are automatically carried out by Oracle, any media failures need to be recovered by the DBA.

Any data file restored from a backup will need media recovery, as will a data file that went offline without a checkpoint being performed. This can happen if a tablespace is taken offline using the IMMEDIATE parameter. If any data file requires recovery the database cannot be opened. Depending on the failure and the recovery procedure the DBA decides to use, it may be possible to recover whilst part of the database is open.

As we discussed earlier, Oracle detects that a file requires media recovery by comparing the checkpoint counter in the file header with the corresponding checkpoint counter in the control file. If these are not the same, recovery is required. When Oracle performs recovery it will start with the lowest checkpoint SCN of the data files being recovered and will continue applying redo until the highest stop SCN is reached. Each redo record is associated with a thread that issued the checkpoint. In an OPS environment, Oracle may need to switch threads in order to apply the redo records in the correct sequence for each block being recovered.

Figure 6.11 shows an example of how this works. In this figure we have redo logs for two threads which need to be applied to a database block. Redo record 1 for thread 1 is applied to block b followed by redo record 2. Redo record 3 cannot be applied until redo record 4 from thread 2 is applied to bring the block up to the correct version number. A thread switch will occur to allow this record to be applied. Another thread switch, back to thread 1, will be performed to apply record 3, bringing the block version number to 9. The last switch to redo thread 2 will then occur so that record 5 can be applied to the block bringing the version number of block b to 10.

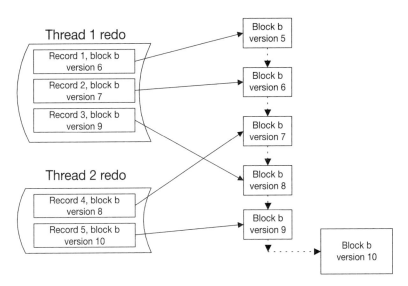

Figure 6.11   Thread switching in an OPS architecture

As can be seen from our example, Oracle may have to apply a single redo log multiple times before recovery is complete.

There are three recovery options available to the DBA whilst performing media recovery:

- **Database recovery** – all, or some, data files can be restored and the entire database recovered.

- **Tablespace recovery** – whilst part of the database is open and available, all data files belonging to a particular tablespace can be recovered.

- **Data file recovery** – in this option a single data file can be recovered whilst the remainder of the database is operational.

When a data file is being recovered, Oracle acquires an exclusive lock on it to avoid other processes, or instances, from trying to recover the same file. This ensures that online files that are in use are not recovered.

In order to recover all lost data up to a point-in-time, the database must be in ARCHIVELOG mode, which is a mandatory requirement from SAP and therefore, by default, it will be in this mode after initial installation of R/3. We will look at how to perform each of the above recovery options using both SAP supplied tools and Oracle tools supplied with the RDBMS later in this chapter.

6.3.5   Resolving ORA and other internal errors

In this section we will discuss some Oracle errors which may be encountered when running SAP R/3. We will look at what each of these errors mean, why they may have occurred and how to resolve them.

Among the most common errors a DBA will encounter on a day-to-day basis are those errors relating to space management and fragmentation. These are caused by the inability of tables to extend due to either lack of space in the tablespace, or excessively fragmented blocks. Similar errors may also occur due to fragmented memory within the shared pool area of the Oracle SGA.

ORA-1545 error

This error indicates a problem with a rollback segment. The actual error text returned is:

`ORA-01545 rollback segment #<name> was not available`

This error message does not tell the DBA why the rollback segment is unavailable but it normally occurs when a rollback segment has a status of NEEDS RECOVERY. The status of rollback segments can be seen by querying the V$ROLLSTAT internal table. Oracle will mark a rollback segment as NEEDS RECOVERY if it is unable to apply all of the undo records from the transaction table for that segment during crash recovery. The best way to detect that this problem is occurring on your database is to set events 10013 and 10015, as discussed earlier in this chapter under the heading **Tracing events**. The events should be enabled in the initialization file. Setting these events causes the transaction table to be dumped to a trace file for all rollback segments before and after recovery. For those roll-back segments where there is a problem applying undo, the before image of the segment will be dumped together with a stack trace. In the dump file there will also be an ORA-1135 error indicating that a data file is offline and needs recovery. The name of the file will appear in the error message text. This file will need media recovery once the problem is resolved.

In order to be able to open the database, the problem rollback segment must be removed from the ROLLBACK_SEGMENTS parameter in the initialization file, and it will then be ignored during the startup checks. One of the possible reasons why undo cannot be applied from a rollback segment could be that a tablespace has been taken offline with the IMMEDIATE parameter, or because the database was mounted and a data file was taken offline. The other reason is that there are corrupt blocks in the rollback segment making it unusable. Events 10013 and 10015 will help you identify which of these problems has occurred and enable you to perform the appropriate recovery. They will also identify the name of the data file causing the problem, as mentioned earlier.

This error can be resolved in one of two ways:

- execute ALTER TABLESPACE <name> ONLINE to bring the tablespace back online. Oracle will then apply the redo and change the status of the rollback segment; or

- drop the tablespace by executing ALTER TABLESPACE <name> DROP which will make the undo data in the rollback segment invalid. Only do this if the tablespace can be rebuilt.

Both of these actions can be performed whilst the database is open.

If neither of these actions can be performed, remove the rollback segment from the initialization file, as described above, and open the database. The Oracle background process SMON will then change the status of the rollback segment from NEEDS RECOVERY to

AVAILABLE after the database has been open for about 30 minutes. Before resetting the status SMON will copy the undo that has not been applied from the rollback segment and write it to a deferred rollback segment as *saveundo* which is stored in the SYSTEM tablespace. The undo will stay there until the offline tablespace is back online and the undo can be applied.

If the SYSTEM rollback segment has an active transaction that cannot be applied because of a tablespace being offline, it will be necessary to restore from a backup. This will only happen if there is only one rollback segment in the entire database.

ORA-1555 error

This error relates to a rollback segment problem that occurs whilst Oracle is trying to provide a read-consistent view to a query. The error text is:

ORA-01555 snapshot too old

In order to be able to resolve this error, we need to understand how Oracle guarantees read-consistency and performs block cleanouts.

Oracle will always provide read-consistency for any queries that are consistent with the time the query began. As a result, a query never sees data that is committed during its execution. Oracle provides this read-consistency by marking the value of the current SCN at the time the query starts. Whilst Oracle is fetching data to satisfy the query, any blocks whose SCN value is greater than the marked SCN value will not be read. Instead Oracle will read the before-image data for the block from the appropriate rollback segment. If the data cannot be found then ORA-1555 is returned. This can happen if the data has been overwritten in the rollback segment, or wraparound has occurred.

The reasons why this error occurs are:

- The rollback segments are too small, which causes Oracle to frequently wraparound in the rollback segment and reuse blocks containing the read-consistent data. This will occur if there are a large number of transactions that commit frequently.

- Corrupted rollback segments can also cause this error if the blocks containing the required data cannot be read.

- Fetch across commits. This is a situation where a query is performing a fetch via a cursor, loops through the data, changes it and then commits. If the cursor then requests blocks that it has committed and the read-consistent data cannot be rebuilt from the rollback segment, ORA-1555 will be reported. The ANSI standard forbids read across commits and recommends that if this situation occurs, the cursor should be closed and reopened. Oracle allows a fetch across commits at the expense of receiving this error.

- Fetch across commits with delayed block cleanout. A delayed block cleanout is a situation where Oracle performs a fast commit on a data block by marking the rollback segment header as committed but not releasing the lock held for that transaction. The next transaction that selects data from the block will release the locks performing a block cleanout. In this case the block cleanout is delayed. If a fetch across commit occurs as described above, whilst querying data from one table and updating records in another table, an ORA-1555 could occur because the block cleanout has not been performed on the table from which we are querying. This will occur if the table from which we are making the initial query was modified by a previous transaction but the blocks had not been cleaned out before we performed the fetch.

ORA-1594 error

The text of this error is:

```
ORA-01594 attempt to wrap into rollback segment <name> extent <num>
which is being freed
```

This means that undo data that has been generated to free a rollback extent is attempting to write the undo to the same extent.

The most likely causes of this error are rollback segments that have very small extent sizes. Oracle will shrink rollback segment extents automatically when a request is made for an extent that is near the end of its free space. If many extents have to be freed, this can generate a large amount of undo causing Oracle to try and write the undo to the same extent it is trying to free. To avoid this problem occurring, make sure your rollback segments have a smaller number of large extents instead of a large number of small extents.

ORA-1652, 1653, 1654 and 1655 errors

These errors relate to Oracle's inability to extend a database object due to lack of free space, or sufficient contiguous free space in a tablespace. This is perhaps the most common error a DBA will encounter. The reason these errors are included in a book about backup and recovery is that, in extreme cases, the author has known catastrophic database failures to occur due to excessive free space fragmentation. By detecting and resolving these errors early, the DBA can avoid total database failures from occurring.

ORA-1652 relates to the inability to extend a temporary segment, ORA-1653 a table, ORA-1654 an index and ORA-1655 a cluster. Each of these errors reports the number of Oracle blocks that were needed and the tablespace in which they were needed. You may find that the tablespace in question has enough free space for the object but that it is not contiguous, in this situation these errors will still occur.

To see the free space in a tablespace you should query the DBA_FREE_SPACE data dictionary table. Each row returned indicates one fragment of free space. The following SQL query will return the rows in order of their BLOCK_ID so it is easier to see if the free space fragments are contiguous:

```
SQL>   select file_id, block_id, blocks, bytes
2 >    from dba_free_space where tablespace_name = 'PSAPBTABD'
3 >    order by block_id;
```

Figure 6.12 shows sample output from executing this command.

FILE_ID	BLOCK_ID	BLOCKS	BYTES
7	10	70	143360
7	80	28	57344
7	210	95	194560

Figure 6.12   Sample free space output

By adding the value in the BLOCK_ID column to that found in the BLOCKS column the result will give you the starting block_id of the next extent. If that extent appears as the next row in the output from the above query then those two free space fragments are contiguous. You can see this in the first two rows of our example in Figure 6.12 above. Adding 10 to 70 in the first row gives a block_id of 80, which happens to be the block_id of the free space fragment in the following row.

In Oracle7, non-contiguous free extents are coalesced automatically by the SMON background process that wakes up every 5 minutes to perform this task. Alternatively the DBA can force the coalesce to take place by executing ALTER TABLESPACE <name> COALESCE. When trying to allocate space to a database object, Oracle will initially try to find exactly the right sized extent, if it cannot it will break up a larger extent. If it cannot do this then it will force a coalesce to take place.

Sometimes the user will get an error on a different tablespace from the one where the database object is being created. This will occur for several reasons:

- A data dictionary table is being updated and there is not enough space for that table to extend.

- An index has to be updated and that index is located in a different tablespace.

- A rollback segment cannot be extended to store the undo data for the transaction.

- Oracle is trying to extend, or create, a temporary segment and there is insufficient space in the temporary tablespace.

To avoid these space management errors occurring, the DBA should ensure all critical R/3 tables and indexes are sized correctly and that the storage parameters used for each table are appropriate for their use.

ORA-7445 error

This error indicates that an operating system exception has occurred and the exception appears as an argument to this error. The error is:

```
[ORA-07445: exception encountered: core dump [var 1] [var 3] [var 4] [var 5]
```

This error will also appear in the Oracle alert log where a trace filename will be shown. In the trace file will be a stack dump and a process state dump for the process that caused the error. This error is normally caused by an Oracle software bug and should be reported to Oracle technical support immediately.

ORA-600 *error*

The ORA-600 error is perhaps most feared by DBAs because it indicates that an internal error has occurred. This error is raised when a sanity check fails within the Oracle code. The ORA-600 is followed by five parameters. The first one indicates the place in the Oracle code where the sanity check failed. Parameters two to five give additional information to Oracle support. For example, if a data file number was found to be out of range an ORA-600 error would be raised and one of the parameters would indicate the number of the file that was being checked.

The error itself does not indicate what the database was doing at the time the error occurred. This information is found from the stack trace dump that is written when the error is flagged. The stack trace will show which processes were running at the time together with the Oracle routines that were active. The stack trace is usually read from the bottom up with the topmost routine being responsible for dumping the stack trace. The process state dump is also written and this shows what objects were being held. A process state dump can be very large with the most useful information being the blocks that the process was manipulating. To make the stack trace human readable, the DBA should format it using the TRCFMT command on the machine where the trace was written.

The following conditions will cause ORA-600 errors to be raised. Also included is an explanation of the information required to investigate each one.

- *Hanging*
  Hanging can be described as a situation where no work is being done. It could be that the machine on which Oracle is running is not responding, the machine is accepting logons but Oracle is not, or the user is connected to Oracle but the session is freezing. In the first case, the systems management team should be consulted to investigate the problem at the machine level. If it is not the machine and Oracle is not accepting connections then it is safe to assume that the Oracle instance is hanging. This usually occurs when Oracle is waiting for some resource to become available.

- *Instance hangs*
  If it is determined that the instance is hanging, then do the following:
  - Check the Oracle alert log for any messages that indicate a background process is stuck or not operating correctly. If such a message is found then corrective action can be taken immediately.
  - Log on to Oracle using Server Manager and connect using the *internal* username. Query the V$LICENCE view and see how many users are connected to the database. Also query the V$SESSION_WAIT view to see what event(s) are being waited on. If, for example, the event LATCH FREE had a particularly high value then perform the following query to see how many events are waiting:

  ```
  select p2, count(*) from v$session_wait where event = 'latch free'
  group by p2;
  ```

  If most of the sessions are waiting on a single latch number, the session holding that latch needs to be identified. Query the V$LATCH view to get the latch name and address (using the LATCH NUMBER returned from the above query in column p2 as a key), and then use the latch address to query the V$LATCHHOLDER view.

- *Session hangs*
  When the offending session has been found, the DBA should do the following:

  - Use either ORADBX or ORADEBUG to attach to the hanging process using the process id identified from the V$LATCHHOLDER view.
  - Perform a process state dump of the process. The resulting trace file may indicate a reason for the hanging.
  - Use an operating system tool such as `truss` or `trace` to see if the process is making any operating system calls. If not the process will be looping tightly within Oracle code. It may also indicate that the process did not return from an operating system call.
  - Use this information to determine where the problem is and why it is occurring, then terminate the process, after leaving the debug program.

- *System crash*
  This is caused by the database crashing due to the failure of a background process. When this occurs do the following:

  - Find out what users were doing at the time and what processes were running on the machine.
  - Check the contents of the alert log and see if any ORA-600 errors have occurred. If so, locate the trace files for them and analyze them further. You may need to set an event(s) as described earlier to investigate this type of problem further.

- *Logical corruptions*
  These are situations where the result of a query returns an incorrect result, or the data as stored is incorrect. Typical examples of such logical corruptions include phantom rows appearing in tables after an update, queries returning different results depending on the optimizer that is used. Such corruptions are very dangerous and difficult to find. The best approach for a DBA to take in these cases is to:

  - Try and reproduce the problem if at all possible.
  - Check the contents of the alert log and look for an ORA-600 error indicating block corruption or some similar problem. If found, analyze the trace files – this may involve setting events (see the earlier discussion on events).

- *Data corruptions*
  This type of corruption includes invalid index entries, data dictionary inconsistencies, and all types of Oracle block format problems. To approach the resolution of such problems:

  - Check the alert log for internal errors such as ORA-600.
  - Analyze the contents of any trace files produced.
  - Dump the contents of the online and archive redo logs corresponding to the time of the corruption. This will include the redo log headers, possibly the data file headers and contents of the control file. Read the section headed **Understanding redo log dumps**, earlier in this chapter, for further advice and help.
  - Hardware diagnostics may also need to be run to locate the source of the corruption.

Resolving block corruptions

Corruption of Oracle blocks can occur due to various reasons and will not normally be noticed until well after the event causing the corruption. For this reason it is necessary to be meticulous in checking all sources of information that can lead to the resolution of persistent block corruptions.

Each Oracle block has a block header containing information about that block. Oracle will use the block header to determine the integrity of the block. One component it checks is the block address, which is a 32-bit integer that stores the file number of where the block is located together with an offset relative to the beginning of that file. Any problems reading this address will cause an ORA-600 error to occur which will appear in the alert log like this:

```
ORA-600 [3339] [var2] [var3] [] [] [] []

ORA-1578 Data block corrupted in file #<num> block #<num>
```

The first variable in the ORA-600 message, [3339], indicates that this is a block corruption message. The second variable, [var2], will contain the block address that was found in the block just read from disk, and the third variable will contain the block address that Oracle expects to find in that data block. The difference between [var2] and [var3] triggers the ORA-600 error. Sometimes [var2] will contain a zero, indicating that this block address was zeroed out, either by the operating system when it attempted to repair the block, or by Oracle when it detected a soft corruption error. In the latter case this zeroing out can be caused by setting event 10210 and/or 10211 (see the earlier discussion on these events and why you may need to set them).

One reason for block corruption is that the block is corrupted in memory and then copied to disk in this state. Setting events 10210 and 10211 will prevent such blocks from being copied to disk. Instead these events will cause the block information to be dumped to trace files and the database will crash. A second reason is that blocks are sometimes written out of sequence and end up in the wrong data files. This occurs when the operating system fails to write the block in the proper location via the *lseek()* system call and is usually found on 32-bit systems that have implemented large UNIX file support, i.e. files greater than 2GB. The operating system has to translate the offset on behalf of Oracle and can occasionally get it wrong!

6.3.6   Recovery within R/3

In this section we look at how to recover the Oracle database using the tools supplied with SAP R/3. We then look at how to recover using Oracle supplied tools that execute outside of the R/3 environment.

In order to be able to restore your lost data within the R/3 system, you need to ensure that your backup was performed using the tools supplied by SAP for this purpose. As described in earlier sections, the Oracle control files, data files and online redo logs are backed up using the BRBACKUP utility. The archived redo logs are backed up using the BRARCHIVE utility. During the recovery process the BRRESTORE utility is used.

When restoring and recovering a database, the DBA must be aware of structural changes that have taken place on the database. Structural changes include the addition of new data files to existing tablespaces, moving or renaming data files, and so on. When any such changes are made, it is essential that they are backed up immediately in case of subsequent failure as the Oracle redo logs do not store the statements required to recreate these changes.

At the beginning of this chapter we discussed what type of recovery can be performed using SAPDBA. To reiterate, SAPDBA can be used to:

- perform full database restore and recovery;

- restore individual files. This means that SAPDBA can be used to restore and recover any data files belonging to the R/3 tablespaces as well as the Oracle SYSTEM tablespace;

- perform point-in-time recovery;

- restore individual control files.

Some error conditions cannot be recovered with SAPDBA. These include:

- the loss of all control files

- structural database changes

- defective online redo logs.

In these cases the DBA must use an Oracle supplied tool, such as RMAN supplied with Oracle8, or Oracle's Enterprise Manager or Server Manager, as supplied with Oracle7.

Recovering the database

The SAPDBA utility is used to restore and recover the entire database. The database can be restored up to the current point in time, or up to an earlier time as specified by the DBA.

To perform the recovery, execute SAPDBA and select option *j – Check (and repair) database* from the initial menu. Figure 6.13 shows the menu that will be displayed at this point.

This menu shows the options available to the DBA for database recovery together with the status of these options. The statuses that may be displayed are as follows:

- *Not finished* – this process has not completed. This status also indicates that the option has not been selected yet.

- *Not needed* – this process is not required.

- *Not allowed* – this process may not be executed.

- *Finished* – this process has completed successfully.

Menu options **a** to **f** allow the DBA to perform the restore and recovery step-by-step whilst option **g** will perform the process automatically. By choosing the automatic option, SAPDBA will guide the DBA through all of the options required, such as stopping the

```
                          Check (and repair) database


                                                              Status

        a — Check      database                               not finished
        b — Find       backup     files                       not finished
        c — Restore    backup     files                       not finished
        d — Find       archive    files                       not finished
        e — Restore    archive    files                       not finished
        f — Recover    database                               not finished

        g — Automatic recovery


        q — Return



        Please select →
```

Figure 6.13   SAPDBA check (and repair) database menu

R/3 system, mounting the appropriate tapes, and so on. The system will always try to use the latest database backup and the latest archived redo logs, which it ascertains from the backup logs created by BRBACKUP and BRARCHIVE. If there are any errors during the restore/recovery process, the *Check (and repair) database* menu will be redisplayed with the status of each option indicated. The DBA will then have the chance of correcting the problem and just running again those options with the status of *not finished*.

If the DBA decides to perform each recovery step manually then he/she will execute each option in the same order as they appear in the menu. The statuses will change dynamically as each option is executed. The entire process is logged to a file in the /oracle/<SID>/sapreorg directory whose name will be in the format <time-stamp>.rcv. Each step will perform a specific action as follows:

a – **Check database.** This step checks the internal Oracle V$ views for any errors that could prevent further recovery. This function can perform two types of tests. The first is an online *quick check* of the database files which is performed whilst the database is open. The idea of this check is to detect the necessity to recover without having to close the database or stop any R/3 processes. On completion of this check the DBA will be asked if a more complete check is required. Before responding positively the DBA must stop R/3. The more comprehensive check, known as a *safe check*, will stop the database and then restart it up to the mount state (but not open). This ensures all information in the V$ views is up to date. The process will then check the status of all control files, data files, tablespaces and redo logs. During this process three possibilities exist:

- An error has occurred on the database that cannot be resolved with SAPDBA. In this case the status of the check database option will be set to *not finished* and the DBA must continue recovery using some other tools.

- No problems are found on the database. The check database option is set to the *finished* status and the remaining options are indicated as *not needed*. No further action needs to be taken by the DBA.

- The check shows some files are damaged. In this event a list of damaged files will be built and the status will be set to *finished*. In this case the next option must be selected to continue.

b – Find backup files. This option is used to select the required backup files that will be needed to restore the damaged files. This option will use the logs created during the backup by the BRBACKUP utility. A further menu option will be displayed as shown in Figure 6.14. Each option works as follows:

- *S – Start finding backup files*. This option must be selected so that SAPDBA can find the required backup files.

- *a – Show the list of damaged files*. This option displays a list of the damaged files together with the appropriate backup where these files can be found.

- *b – Show the list of backup files*. This option can be used to view the location of a backup for a particular damaged file.

- *c – Select a backup file for restore*. This option allows the DBA to select a different backup from which to restore a lost file.

```
                          Find backup files


    S — Start finding backup files

    a — Show the list of damaged files
    b — Show the list of backup files

    c — Select a backup file for restore
    d — Select a BRBACKUP run for restore

    q — Return



    Please select →
```

Figure 6.14   SAPDBA find backup files menu

- *d – Select a BRBACKUP run for restore*. This option allows the DBA to select which backup to restore from for every damaged file. This option is used if the DBA does not want to restore files from different backup runs.

  Selecting *q – Return* will cause the previous menu to be displayed and the status of the option will be set to finished.

c – **Restore backup files**. This option will copy the damaged file(s) from the selected backups to their correct destinations using the BRRESTORE utility. Any files with the same name in the same destination directories will be overwritten. The DBA will be given the option of deciding if the overwrite should take place. Selecting the *no* option will terminate the restore process. This option will display an additional menu from which various restore options may be changed. Normally this will not be required since these options are automatically set from the backup logs. Various checks are performed, including checking to make sure there is sufficient disk space to perform the restore. If not, a message is issued and the restore is paused. Once the DBA has resolved the disk space problem, the restore process can be continued. **Restoring with this function is not allowed if a structural change has been made to the database since the backup was taken, unless this structural change is reflected in the backup being used**. On successful completion, the option status is set to *finished*.

d – **Find archive files**. This option works in a similar way to the *Find backup files* option. This item will search for the location of the backup archived redo logs by looking in the log file created by BRARCHIVE when they were backed up. This option displays three additional menu options:

- *Specify first archive file to be found/restored (Current setting: <num>)*. The number in brackets indicates the first archived log file sequence number needed for recovery. The DBA can change this option if necessary. Change with caution because specifying an incorrect number can cause the recovery to fail.

- *Show the list of archive files*. This option displays a list of the archived redo logs required to perform the recovery.

- *Start finding archive files*. This function must be selected to start the process to locate the backups where the archived files are stored. Not only will the backup devices be searched, but the archived redo log directory on disk will also be searched in case an archived redo log is required that has not yet been backed up.

  Returning to the previous menu will set the status of the option to *finished* on successful completion.

e – **Restore archive files**. Selecting this option will cause the archived redo logs to be copied from the backup device(s) to their proper locations on disk. Once again the BRRESTORE utility will be used for this purpose. It is not necessary to perform this function if the required archived redo logs are still on disk. It is also possible to perform the restore of these files whilst the recovery is in process. If the directory becomes full, the process will remove any archived redo logs that have already been used.

f – Recover database. Once all previous options have been executed this option can be selected to start the recovery of the database. During the recovery process various messages will be displayed. If a particular archived redo log is required and cannot be found, the DBA will be prompted to restore it before recovery can proceed. On successful completion, the status will be set to *finished* and the database will be reopened.

There are additional database restore/recovery options available. These are accessed from the SAPDBA main menu option *k – Restore/recovery*. The menu that is displayed is shown in Figure 6.15. We will discuss the first two options from this menu here, and the remaining options will be discussed in the following sections on tablespace and data file recovery.

The first two options are as follows:

a – Full restore (incl. redo logs and control files). This option completely resets the database to the state it was in at the time of the full offline backup used for the restore. The BRRESTORE utility is used to restore **all** data files, control files, online redo logs, and mirror copies. This option displays two further menu options:

- *a – Restore database and startup open (no recovery possible)*. This has the effect of restoring and recovering the database to the same state as at the time the backup was taken. There is no further possibility for recovery. Any backups taken since the date of the backup used for the restore are of no use. **Problems with archived log sequence numbers and BRBACKUP/BRARCHIVE logs may occur after using this option. The SAPnet website should be consulted for further information (see *http://sapnet.sap-ag.de*).**

- *b – Restore database and startup mount (for manual recovery (using backup controlfile))*. This option will restore the complete database but will not open it (it will be in the

```
                           Restore/recovery


  a — Full restore
      (incl. redo logs and control files)
  b — Full restore and recovery
      (excl. redo logs)

  c — Restore one tablespace
  d — Restore individual file(s)

  q — Return

  Please select   →
```

Figure 6.15   SAPDBA restore and recovery menu

mounted state on successful completion of this option). The DBA will need to perform further recovery using the RECOVER   DATABASE   USING   BACKUP CONTROLFILE option within the Oracle Server Manager. Executing the functions on the check (and repair) database menu can also perform this function.

b – **Full restore and recovery (excl. redo logs)**. This option can be used to perform recovery to a specific point-in-time (rather than to the current point-in-time as described earlier). This option will display an additional menu, which can be seen in Figure 6.16. The options are as follows:

- *A – Select a full online/offline backup*. The DBA uses this option to specify the full backup that should be used to restore/recover from.

- *b – Recover until*. This option is used to specify the date and time up to which the full recovery should be performed. The default is *now*, which will recover the database up to the current time. The format to be used when entering the date and time is YYY-MM-DD HH.MM.SS. Remember that all of the data backed up between the recovery date and time specified and the current time will be of no use after recovery is complete. Also check whether there have been any structural changes made to the database since the date and time of the backup and the recovery time specified.

- *c- Show status*. This option will show which backup has been selected together with the archived redo logs that will be applied. It will also show whether recovery will be possible. If not, it may be due to structural changes made to the

```
                        Full restore and recovery


        DATABASE STATE    : Database open
        RESTORE / RECOVER: disallowed (see status)


                                          Current setting

        A — Select a full online/offline backup
        b — Recover until                              now
        c — Show status
        D — Restore and recover

        q — Return



        Please select →
```

Figure 6.16   SAPDBA full restore and recovery menu

database that cannot be recovered because such changes are not logged in the redo logs.

- *D – Restore and recover.* Selecting this option starts the restore/recovery process. A log file will be created in the `/oracle/<SID>/sapreorg` directory and will be called `<timestamp>.rsn`, for recoveries up to the current point-in-time, or `<timestamp>.rsp`, for recoveries to an earlier point-in-time.

Recovering individual tablespaces

To recover individual tablespaces it is necessary to perform two steps. First, the data files for the chosen tablespace must be copied from the backup back to their original locations on disk. Second, the archived redo log data needs to be applied.

To perform the first step, select option *k – Restore/recovery* from the SAPDBA main menu. The menu that is now displayed is shown in Figure 6.15. From this menu select option *c – Restore one tablespace*, specify the tablespace you wish to restore and the backup from which the data files should be copied. A new menu will appear allowing you to change the restore parameters. These will normally be left to the defaults so select *q – Return to restore process and continue* which will then copy the files from the backup to their correct location on disk. The database will be stopped for the restore to take place and will remain closed after it has completed successfully. If you need to keep the database online during a tablespace recovery you should use the Oracle tools supplied with the database instead (see later).

The second step is to apply the redo log data to the restored files. This has to be performed from the SAPDBA main menu by selecting option *j – Check (and repair) database*. Figure 6.13 shows the menu that will be displayed at this point. Use the *recover database* option from the *Check (and repair) database* menu to perform the recovery.

Recovering individual data files

To recover individual data files, as opposed to all data files for a chosen tablespace, select option *d – Restore individual file(s)* from the *Restore/recovery* menu. A second menu is displayed as shown in Figure 6.17.

The procedure is as follows:

- Select option *a – File type*, this will display a third menu as seen in Figure 6.18.

- As you can see from this menu, you can restore other types of database files as well as non-database files. If restoring non-database files it is sufficient to simply restore them from a backup. If restoring database files it may be necessary to perform a recovery step as well, as is the case when restoring data files. To restore data files select option *b – Data files* from the menu then select option *q – Return* to go back to the previous menu (Figure 6.17).

- Next select option *b – BRBACKUP run* to select the backup from which the required data file(s) are to be copied. If copying other file types you may not need to select this option. In this case the status of the option will be set to *<no need for selection>*.

```
                         Restore individual file(s)


      a — File type       : Offline redo logs
      b — BRBACKUP run     : <no need for selection>
      c — Enter/show files : <no selection>

      S — Start BRRESTORE

      q — Return


      Please select →
```

Figure 6.17   SAPDBA restore individual file(s)

- Select option *c – Enter/show files*. A list of files available from the backup selected in option *b* will be displayed. Select one or more files from this list, their status will be set to *Res yes* indicating that they will be restored.

- To start the restore select option *S – Start BRRESTORE*. As this option indicates, the BRRESTORE utility will be used to copy the chosen file(s) from the backup device(s). If files with the same name already exist, you will be prompted to indicate whether you want them overwritten or not. Selecting the *no* option will terminate the restore.

- During the restore, various messages will be displayed including prompts for the operator to mount the required tape(s). All activities are logged to a file called `<timestamp>.dba` in the `/oracle/<SID>/sapreorg` directory.

- On successful completion of the restore, the recovery process will have to be started from the *Check (and repair)* database menu.

Restoring the control file

To restore the control file use the same menu option used to restore data files, as described in the previous section. The procedure is as follows:

- Select option *a – File type*, this will display a third menu as seen in Figure 6.18.

- Select option *c – Control file* from the menu then select option *q – Return* to go back to the previous menu (Figure 6.17).

- Next select option *b – BRBACKUP run* to select the backup from which the control file is to be copied.

- Select option *c – Enter/show files*. A list of files available from the backup selected in option *b* will be displayed. Select the control file and its status will be set to *Res yes*.

```
                    Select file type for restore

NOTE: Profiles and log files can only be restored from a tape!

   Current selection: <no selection>

   a — Non-database files
   b — Data files
   c — Control file
   d — Online redo logs
   e — Offline redo logs
   f — Oracle profile (init.ora)
   g — BRBACKUP/BRARCHIVE log file
   h — Main SAPDBA log file
   i — Summary BRBACKUP/BRARCHIVE log file
   j — Detail BRBACKUP/BRARCHIVE log file

   q — Return


   Please select →
```

Figure 6.18   SAPDBA file selection menu

- To start the restore select option *S – Start BRRESTORE*. As this option indicates, the BRRESTORE utility will be used to copy the chosen file from the backup device. If the control file already exists on disk, you will be prompted to indicate whether you want it overwritten or not. Selecting the *no* option will terminate the restore.

- During the restore, various messages will be displayed including prompts for the operator to mount the required tape. All activities are logged to a file called <timestamp>.dba in the /oracle/<SID>/sapreorg directory.

- On successful completion of the restore, you will need to perform a recovery. Because you have restored an older control file you cannot use the SAP tools to perform this recovery, therefore you will need to use Oracle's Server Manager and execute the RECOVER DATABASE USING BACKUP CONTROLFILE command.

6.3.7   Recovery within Oracle

We will now consider how to recover an R/3 database using the Oracle supplied tools. You will need to perform recoveries with these tools if any of the following conditions are true:

- ALL control files have been lost (main control file and mirror copies);

- there have been structural changes to the database;

- an online redo log is defective.

Of course you can also use the Oracle tools instead of the SAP ones to perform all types of recovery. By default the R/3 database is running in ARCHIVELOG mode which gives you more recovery options and more flexibility as to how you recover. Some types of recovery can be performed online, others offline. When performing a database level recovery the database must be offline, when recovering a tablespace the database must be online, unless the SYSTEM tablespace is being recovered when the database must be offline. When recovering a data file the database can be either on- or offline.

Recovering the database

To recover the Oracle database requires the use of the RECOVER DATABASE command within the Oracle Server Manager tool. This command is available in both Oracle7 and Oracle8. Alternatively, an Oracle8 database can be recovered using Oracle Recovery Manager (RMAN) which is the preferred tool for backing up and recovering Oracle8. We will use RECOVER DATABASE to illustrate the recovery techniques and then discuss how to perform recoveries using RMAN.

A single Oracle process is responsible for performing recovery. This process reads the relevant redo logs and applies the redo data to the data files that require recovery. It is also possible to use a parallel recovery option, introduced in Oracle 7.1. When using parallel recovery, Server Manager will pass the redo to be applied to several recovery processes and, in turn, these processes apply the redo to the relevant data files. Each process recovers a specific set of data blocks and is not dedicated to recovering a particular file.

Two types of database recovery can be performed. *Complete recovery* will restore the database without loss of data assuming all redo logs, data files and control files are available. If an archived or online redo log is lost, then only *incomplete recovery* can be performed up to the point of the lost redo log. In this situation data will be lost. There is no reason why this situation should occur if an adequate backup strategy is put in place.

To perform a complete database recovery to the current point-in-time the procedure is:

- Restore all data files and archived redo logs. This can be done by either using a UNIX command such as tar or cpio, or using the SAP BRRESTORE utility to copy the files from the relevant backup. Remember in order to use BRRESTORE you must have backed up the files using BRBACKUP and BRARCHIVE.

- Mount the Oracle database using the command startup restrict mount.

- Query the V$DATAFILE view to see if any data files requiring recovery are offline. If they are, bring them back online with the command ALTER DATABASE '<data file-name>' ONLINE.

- If you are restoring a data file to a different location from where it was originally (possibly due to a disk crash) then execute the command ALTER DATABASE RENAME FILE

'<old filename>' TO '<new filename>'. The <old filename> and <new file-name> parameters must include the full path name. This command will change the location of the file in the control file.

- Execute the Server Manager program in line mode and enter RECOVER DATABASE. Oracle will prompt for each redo log to be applied and will supply the required log sequence number. To accept it simply press the <Enter> key. Alternatively use the following format of the command, RECOVER AUTOMATIC DATABASE, which will apply the redo logs without prompting.

- To use this type of recovery the data files to be recovered must be online, all required archived redo log files must be available on disk and the current control file must be available.

To perform incomplete recovery use **one** of the following commands from within Server Manager (line mode), after having restored the relevant data files and archived redo log files, mounted the database and brought any offline data files back online as described above:

- RECOVER DATABASE UNTIL CANCEL – this will allow you to apply the redo logs one log at a time until the CANCEL command is entered. You will need to determine how many logs you want to apply to get you to the recovery point you want to be at.

- RECOVER DATABASE UNTIL TIME '<time>' – this will perform point-in-time recovery up to the time specified. The format of <time> is YYYY-MM-DD:HH:MI:SS. Any date and time prior to the current date and time can be used.

- RECOVER DATABASE UNTIL CHANGE <num> – this will recover the database up to the SCN number specified in place of <num>. Note that all records with an SCN value **lower** than the specified SCN will be applied. Oracle will ensure all redo records are applied to recover the database to a consistent state.

- If you have restored a control file from a backup then you must use the USING BACKUP CONTROLFILE parameter with any of the above commands.

When performing *incomplete recovery* the database must be in the mounted state. After recovery has completed the database must then be opened with the command ALTER DATABASE OPEN RESETLOGS which will reset the redo logs. **It is essential to perform a full offline or online backup of the database after opening with this option**. Any backup redo logs will now be useless for recovery and can safely be overwritten. Any data files that are offline during the *incomplete recovery* will not be recovered. This is OK if the data files are offline due to the tablespace being taken offline using the NORMAL parameter. If the tablespace was taken offline using any other parameter, then it must be brought back online prior to running the recovery otherwise it will not be able to be recovered and will have to be dropped, with a loss of data. It is wise, therefore, to query the V$DATAFILE view before performing the recovery to see which data files are offline. This view can be queried with the database in the mounted state. Data files can also be brought online with the database in the mounted state using the ALTER DATABASE '<data filename>' ONLINE.

Recovering individual tablespaces

To recover individual tablespaces the RECOVER TABLESPACE command is used whilst the database is open, the tablespace to be recovered must be offline and the current control file must be available. As the SYSTEM tablespace cannot be taken offline, recovery cannot be performed on this tablespace using the RECOVER TABLESPACE command.

The procedure for performing tablespace recovery is as follows:

- Take the tablespace to be recovered offline with ALTER TABLESPACE <tablespace name> OFFLINE.

- Restore the data file(s) that require recovery from the backup. You may also need to restore the archived redo logs as well. This can be done by either using a UNIX command such as tar or cpio, or using the SAP BRRESTORE utility to copy the files from the relevant backup. Remember in order to use BRRESTORE you must have backed up the files using BRBACKUP and BRARCHIVE.

- If you are restoring a data file to a different location from where it was originally (possibly due to a disk crash) then execute the command ALTER DATABASE RENAME FILE '<old filename>' TO '<new filename>'. The <old filename> and <new filename> parameters must include the full path name. This command will change the location of the file in the control file.

- Recover the tablespace with the command RECOVER TABLESPACE <tablespace name>.

- Bring the tablespace back online using the command ALTER TABLESPACE <tablespace name> ONLINE.

Recovering individual data files

To recover individual data files use the RECOVER DATAFILE command. Online and offline data file recovery is possible as long as media recovery locks can be applied. Data file recovery is not possible for the SYSTEM tablespace. The current control file must be available and the data file(s) to be recovered must be taken offline when performing online recovery.

The procedure for performing online data file recovery is as follows:

- Mount the database, but do not open it yet! Use the command startup mount.

- Take all damaged data files offline. Use this command for each data file ALTER DATABASE DATAFILE '<data filename>' OFFLINE.

- Open the database with ALTER DATABASE OPEN.

- Restore the data files requiring recovery from the backup. You may also need to restore required archived redo log files as well.

- If you are restoring a data file to a different location from where it was originally (possibly due to a disk crash) then execute the command ALTER DATABASE RENAME FILE

'<old filename>' TO '<new filename>'. The <old filename> and <new file-name> parameters must include the full path name. This command will change the location of the file in the control file.

- Recover the data file(s) using the command RECOVER DATAFILE '<data file-name>','<data filename>' etc.

- After successful completion of the recovery bring the data file(s) online using ALTER DATABASE DATAFILE '<data filename>' ONLINE.

To perform offline data file recovery the procedure is:

- Restore the data files requiring recovery from the backup. You may also need to restore required archived redo log files as well.

- If you are restoring a data file to a different location from where it was originally (pos-sibly due to a disk crash) then execute the command ALTER DATABASE RENAME FILE '<old filename>' TO '<new filename>'. The <old filename> and <new file-name> parameters must include the full path name. This command will change the location of the file in the control file.

- Mount the database with the command startup restrict mount.

- Because the database is closed the data files to be recovered can either be online or offline. Use the command ALTER DATABASE DATAFILE '<data filename>' ONLINE or ALTER DATABASE DATAFILE '<data filename>' OFFLINE.

- Recover the data file(s) using the command RECOVER DATAFILE '<data file-name>','<data filename>' etc.

- If the data file was offline during recovery then bring it back online. Use the command ALTER DATABASE DATAFILE '<data filename>' ONLINE.

- Open the database using the command ALTER DATABASE OPEN.

It is possible to recover data files in parallel using multiple Server Manager sessions.

Whenever you change the structure of a database ensure you always backup the new data file(s) and the control file. If a failure occurs before you can backup these changes then it is possible to recreate the data file(s). The procedure to do this is:

- Execute the following command ALTER DATABASE CREATE DATAFILE '<data file-name>'. This command can be used to create data files for the SYSTEM tablespace as long as the database is running in ARCHIVELOG mode.

- Recover the database using the RECOVER DATABASE command. This will apply all redo records to the empty data file created.

Restoring the control file

When performing a recovery, it is recommended to always use the current control file. If this is not possible then the options are to either restore the control file from a backup or to create a new one. Either way, you will need to perform a recovery once the control file has been restored using the command RECOVER DATABASE USING BACKUP CONTROLFILE. You should only create a new control file if you do not have a backup copy.

To create a new control file use the CREATE CONTROLFILE command. This command is most commonly used to alter the values for the MAXDATAFILES and MAXLOGFILES parameters that are specified at database creation time. This avoids having to recreate the database simply to change these parameters.

To create a new control file follow this procedure:

1. Startup the Oracle instance but do not mount it. Use the command startup nomount.

2. Create the script containing the SQL statement to create the control file. To do this execute the following command ALTER DATABASE BACKUP CONTROLFILE TO TRACE. This will write the SQL statement to a trace file contained in the directory /oracle/<SID>/saptrace.

3. Run the SQL script created in step 2. This will create a new control file. The script will also perform a database recovery and open the database.

Incremental recovery

Using the Oracle Import utility allows the database to be recovered from an *incremental backup* taken with the Oracle Export utility. Performing incremental backups with Oracle Export was described in Chapter 5.

Import is executed in the same way as Export. It is run from the UNIX command line together with various parameters. These parameters can also be supplied from a parameter file so that the recovery process can be run from a shell script. Before we look at how to perform recoveries from a logical backup, we will take at look at the parameters that can be used with Import.

The Import parameters are:

- **USERID** – the username/password of the Oracle user performing the Import. This should be the R/3 user that owns the database objects.

- **BUFFER** – the size of the data buffer used to fetch the rows. This should be set to a value greater than 64000 bytes.

- **FILE** – the name of the output file that contains the logical backup. This defaults to expdat.dmp.

- **SHOW** – by setting this parameter to *yes*, Import will simply display the contents of the logical backup without restoring it. The parameter defaults to *no*.

- **IGNORE** – by setting this parameter to *no*, if an object already exists creation errors will be ignored and the data will be imported. This parameter defaults to *yes*.

- **GRANTS** – this parameter determines whether grants will be imported. Defaults to *yes*.

- **INDEXES** – this parameter determines whether indexes will be created. Defaults to *yes*.

- **ROWS** – this parameter determines whether the data will be imported. Defaults to *yes*.

- **FULL** – when set to *yes* the entire contents of the import file will be imported. Defaults to *no*.

- **FROMUSER** – a list of user names whose objects exist in the import file. This parameter is not used when recovering an R/3 database.

- **TOUSER** – a list of user names to whom data is imported. This parameter is not used when recovering an R/3 database.

- **TABLES** – a list of table names to import.

- **RECORDLENGTH** – the length, in bytes, of each record in the import file. This is only used if the operating system you are running Import on is different to the one that created the Export file. This will not normally be the case.

- **INCTYPE** – defines the type of incremental import. Valid values are `SYSTEM` and `RESTORE`. `SYSTEM` will rebuild the database objects, `RESTORE` will import the data.

- **COMMIT** – this parameter determines when Import will commit the data to the database. By default the parameter is set to *no* which will cause a commit to occur after importing each table. Setting this parameter to *yes* will cause a commit to occur after each array insert. The size of the array is determined by the **BUFFER** parameter.

- **PARFILE** – the name of the file containing the parameter values. The author recommends using this file to simplify the R/3 restore procedure.

In Chapter 5 we discussed the different types of backups that can be performed using Export – COMPLETE, CUMULATIVE, and INCREMENTAL. To perform an import from an incremental export do the following:

- Using the *most recent* export file (it does not matter whether it is a COMPLETE, CUMULATIVE or INCREMENTAL backup), restore the database object definitions with the command

  ```
  imp <username>/<password> INCTYPE=system TABLES=<table name(s)to
  restore> FILE=<export filename>.
  ```

- Bring the necessary rollback segments online.

- Import the most recent COMPLETE export file using the command

  ```
  imp <username>/<password> INCTYPE=restore TABLES=<table name(s) to
  restore> FILE=<export filename>
  ```

- Import, in chronological order, all of the CUMULATIVE backups since the most recent COMPLETE backup. If no CUMULATIVE backups were performed then go onto the next step. To perform the import execute the command

  ```
  imp <username>/<password> INCTYPE=restore TABLES=<table name(s) to
  restore> FILE=<export filename>
  ```

- Finally, import, in chronological order, all of the INCREMENTAL backups taken since the most recent CUMULATIVE (or COMPLETE) backup using the command

```
imp <username>/<password> INCTYPE=restore TABLES=<table name(s) to
restore> FILE=<export filename>.
```

Using RMAN for recovery

If you are running R/3 with an Oracle8 database and you do not backup your database using the SAP supplied tools, Oracle recommends you use Oracle Recovery Manager (RMAN) to manage the recovery of your database. The process of recovery with RMAN is similar to the process used with SAPDBA. First you must restore the required database files and then perform a recovery. RMAN maintains details of all backups performed against Oracle8 within the RMAN Recovery Catalog. This catalog is a set of tables stored in an Oracle8 database separate from the database being backed up. Alternatively, instead of using a database-based catalog, it is possible for RMAN to write the information into the current control file. One disadvantage with this approach is that, at the time of writing, it is not possible to perform point-in-time recovery.

Restoring files with RMAN

When restoring files with RMAN, it is possible to either restore them from a backup set, or from copies that are already on disk. When we discussed how to backup your database with RMAN we talked about *image copies* of data files (see Chapter 5). These are held on disk and can be switched to, rather than being restored from a backup set. It is also possible to restore the files to a different location if, for example, you experience a disk crash. This is achieved by using the SET NEWNAME command within RMAN.

It is also possible to restore archived redo logs from backup sets. This is not mandatory however, as RMAN will automatically restore them as part of the recovery process. If, however, you want to speed up the recovery process, the author recommends you pre-restore the archived redo logs if necessary, from your backup sets.

To determine which backup sets to use, RMAN reads the recovery catalog (or control file if no catalog is available). RMAN will give preference to copies on disk because recovery will be faster, so where there is a choice of going to a backup set for a file or using an on-disk copy, RMAN will always select the latter.

By default, RMAN will always restore files to their current location as specified in the recovery catalog, overwriting any files with the same name that are already present. This will not happen if the SET NEWNAME command has been run beforehand. In this case, the restored files are considered file copies, and you must perform a switch to make them the current files. When restoring a control file you must specify a destination. The previous control file will be overwritten if it exists. Archived redo logs are restored to the destination as specified in the Oracle initialization file. You can copy them to a different location if you wish, although with R/3 it is not recommended unless you have lost the original disk on which your archived redo logs are normally located. Again, any archived redo logs that already exist with the same name will be overwritten.

If you have taken incremental backups with RMAN then you should restore the level 0 (zero) backup set, **not the backup sets containing the incremental backups**. Incremental backups at levels greater than 0 (zero) are restored during the recovery.

If you do not specify set newname when restoring files, then either the database must be closed, or the files must be offline. If the entire database is to be restored it must be closed.

Recovering with RMAN

There are three types of recovery that can be performed with RMAN:

- *Recover database* – which will recover an entire database. The database must be mounted but not open.

- *Recover tablespace* – which will recover individual tablespaces.

- *Recover datafile* – which recovers individual data files.

To perform tablespace and data file recovery, the database must be mounted. If the database is open then the tablespace and data files must be taken offline.

Database recovery with RMAN

To recover a database using RMAN perform the following procedure:

- Start the database, but do not mount or open it. Use the command startup nomount.

- Start RMAN. Make sure the recovery catalog is available if applicable.

- Assign the backup device channel so RMAN knows where to get the backup set. Use this command:

  allocate channel dev1 type '<backup device name>';

- Mount the database using the command SQL 'ALTER DATABASE MOUNT';

- Restore the database and recover it using these commands:

  RESTORE DATABASE;

  RECOVER DATABASE;

- Open the database using the command SQL 'ALTER DATABASE OPEN';

- Close the communication channel using the command

  RELEASE CHANNEL DEV1;

Figure 6.19 shows these commands as entered at the RMAN command line. You can also save these commands as a script and store them in the RMAN recovery catalog for later execution.

```
RMAN> run {
2> allocate channel dev1 type 'tape';
3> sql 'alter database mount';
2> restore database;
3> recover database;
4> sql 'alter database open';
5> release channel dev1;
6> }
```

Figure 6.19   Database recovery with RMAN

This procedure will restore and recover the database to the current point-in-time. If you need to restore to an earlier point-in-time then you need to use the SET UNTIL TIME command, which is shown in Figure 6.20. This figure shows an RMAN dialog that recovers a database to January 2, 1999 at 12:00. Take particular note of the format of the date and time when using this command. Figure 6.20 also shows an example of a control file being restored as part of the recovery process. In this case, when we open the database we have to use the RESETLOGS parameter.

Tablespace recovery with RMAN

To recover an individual tablespace whilst the database is open perform the following procedure: -

• Assign a channel to the backup device

```
ALLOCATE CHANNEL DEV1 TYPE '<BACKUP DEVICE NAME>';
```

• Take the tablespace offline

```
SQL 'ALTER TABLESPACE <TABLESPACE NAME> OFFLINE IMMEDIATE' ;
```

```
RMAN> run {
2> allocate channel dev1 type 'tape';
3> set until time 'Jan 2 1999 12:00:00'
4> restore controlfile;
1> sql 'alter database mount';
2> restore database;
3> recover database;
4> sql 'alter database open resetlogs';
5> release channel dev1;
6> }
```

Figure 6.20   Restoring to an earlier point-in-time

- Restore and recover the tablespace

  ```
  RESTORE TABLESPACE <TABLESPACE NAME> ;
  ```

  ```
  RECOVER TABLESPACE <TABLESPACE NAME> ;
  ```

- Bring tablespace back online

  ```
  SQL 'ALTER TABLESPACE <TABLESPACE NAME> ONLINE';
  ```

- Release communication channel

  ```
  RELEASE CHANNEL DEV1;
  ```

  Figure 6.21 shows the RMAN dialog.

```
RMAN> run {
2> allocate channel dev1 type 'tape';
3> sql 'alter tablespace <tablespace name> offline';
4> restore tablespace <tablespace name>;
5> recover tablespace <tablespace name>;
6> sql 'alter tablespace <tablespace name> online';
7> release channel dev1;
8> }
```

Figure 6.21   Recovering a tablespace using RMAN

Data file recovery with RMAN

To recover an individual data file whilst the database is open perform the following procedure:

- Assign a channel to the backup device

  ```
  ALLOCATE CHANNEL DEV1 TYPE '<backup device name>';
  ```

- Take the data file offline

  ```
  SQL 'ALTER DATABASE DATAFILE <data filename> offline' ;
  ```

- Restore and recover the data file

  ```
  RESTORE DATAFILE <data filename> ;
  ```

  ```
  RECOVER DATAFILE <data filename> ;
  ```

- Bring data file back online

  ```
  SQL 'ALTER DATABASE DATAFILE <data filename> online' ;
  ```

- Release communication channel

  ```
  RELEASE CHANNEL DEV1;
  ```

Figure 6.22 shows the RMAN dialog.

```
RMAN> run {
2> allocate channel dev1 type 'tape';
3> sql 'alter database datafile <data filename> offline';
4> restore datafile <data filename>;
5> recover datafile <data filename>;
6> sql 'alter database datafile <data filename> online';
7> release channel dev1;
8> }
```

Figure 6.22   Recovering a data file with RMAN

7 Disaster recovery considerations

In this chapter we discuss further options available for guaranteeing R/3 system availability. These options are particularly valuable in a disaster recovery situation and will have an impact on your backup and recovery strategy.

7.1 Hot standby database

As of Oracle7 release 7.3, Oracle Corporation officially supports the concept and implementation of a hot standby database to provide extra resilience in case of catastrophic failure of the production Oracle system. A hot standby database, as defined by Oracle, is a copy of the production database system residing on another machine. This database is kept in step by the constant application of the archived redo logs made available from the production system. If the production system should fail, it is possible to switch over to the standby database within a short amount of time, thereby minimizing downtime of the SAP R/3 system.

In this section we will discuss the standby database architecture and show how SAP supports this architecture with BRBACKUP and BRARCHIVE. SAP expects customers who use this type of configuration with their R/3 system to bear the full responsibility of configuring it and maintaining it.

7.1.1 The advantages and disadvantages of a hot standby database

Before deciding whether implementing a hot standby database scenario is appropriate for your site, it is worth considering the advantages and disadvantages of doing so.

The advantages of this architecture are:

- A reduced R/3 system failure rate. The production R/3 system is duplicated on another machine, which may be situated in a different building from the main system, or located on a disaster recovery site.

- The amount of downtime during a failure is reduced. To effect a switch over, the hot standby database must have the last redo log records applied to it, then it can be opened. This is far quicker than restoring data files and performing a recovery in order to restart the production system.

- Backups of your production system can be executed from the hot standby machine reducing the amount of load on your production machine. In a 24x7 environment, database backups will consume a large amount of CPU processing power, reducing throughput for your online production users.

The disadvantages of a hot standby database architecture are:

- It is expensive! Your hot standby machine will contain an exact duplicate of your production system.

- It places a high administrative burden on the DBA. The DBA must set up the hot standby database and then continue to maintain it from there. If any structural changes are made to the production database, the same changes must be applied to the hot standby database. If this is not done, subsequent applications of the redo logs will fail.

- So that the hot standby machine can automatically assume responsibility for running the R/3 system in the event of a failure of the production machine, switchover software, and possibly hardware, will be required. This can be implemented via UNIX shell scripts but they involve a lot of programming and maintenance.

7.1.2   The hot standby database architecture

Figure 7.1 shows the architecture of the hot standby database.

This figure shows two machines. The primary machine is the production R/3 system, the secondary machine is the hot standby database, which is an exact copy of the production database. The database on the primary machine is fully open and accepting SQL requests from R/3 production users, whilst on the secondary machine Oracle is mounted in a 'standby state'. This means that the database on this machine is in a constant recovery state. As new redo logs are archived on the primary machine, they must be copied to the secondary machine and 'recovered' on the hot standby database.

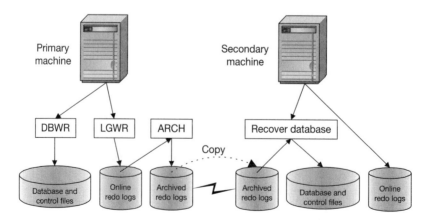

Figure 7.1   Oracle hot standby database architecture

A brief outline of how to create a hot standby database environment follows:

- On the primary machine backup the initialization file (`init<SID>.ora`) and all database data files. Create the standby control file using the command `ALTER DATABASE CREATE STANDBY CONTROLFILE AS '<filename>'`. Archive to current redo log using the command `ALTER SYSTEM ARCHIVE LOG CURRENT`.

- Copy these files, together with the archived redo logs, to the secondary machine containing the hot standby database.

- On the secondary machine restore the files and recover them using the following commands;

  ```
  startup nomount pfile=<standby control file name>

  RECOVER STANDBY DATABASE
  ```

- Mount the standby database using the command `ALTER DATABASE MOUNT STANDBY DATABASE`.

- Leave the hot standby database in recovery mode.

- For full details on how to implement a hot standby database, please refer to the Oracle documentation set.

After the hot standby database has been set up it will then need to be maintained. As a new archived redo log file is created on the production system, it should be copied to the secondary machine and applied to the database. You must remember that the hot standby database is only as current as the last 'recovered' transaction in the last archived redo log that was applied to it from the production system. If the archive stream is interrupted at the production database, the hot standby database must be rebuilt. For example, if a media recovery is performed on the production database, archiving is stopped. In this case, the hot standby database would have to be rebuilt from a fresh backup copy by following the steps described above.

Because the archived redo logs is the mechanism for maintaining the hot standby database, certain actions that are performed on the production system will **not** be automatically propagated to the hot standby. For example, any structural changes such as adding a new data file will not be propagated although subsequent redo for the new data file will be. In this case the DBA must create the data file on the hot standby database as well, taking care to make sure it is in the same location on the secondary machine and of the same size.

To help you, here is a list of the commands that can be run on the primary database that **will be propagated** via the archived redo logs to the hot standby database:

- `sqlldr direct=false` (using the `RECOVERABLE` option)

- `ALTER CLUSTER`

- `ALTER DATABASE DATAFILE AUTOEXTEND, DATAFILE END BACKUP, DATAFILE OFFLINE, DATAFILE ONLINE, DATAFILE RESIZE`

- ALTER FUNCTION

- ALTER INDEX, ALTER INDEX RECOVERABLE

- ALTER PACKAGE, PROCEDURE, PROFILE, RESOURCE COST, ROLE, ROLLBACK SEGMENT, SEQUENCE

- ALTER SNAPSHOT, SNAPSHOT LOG

- ALTER TABLE

- ALTER TABLESPACE COALESCE, DEFAULT STORAGE, OFFLINE, ONLINE, PERMANENT, READ WRITE, READ ONLY, TEMPORARY

- ALTER TRIGGER, USER, VIEW

- ANALYZE, AUDIT, COMMIT

- CREATE CLUSTER

- CREATE DATABASE, LINK, FUNCTION

- CREATE INDEX, CREATE INDEX RECOVERABLE

- CREATE PACKAGE, PACKAGE BODY, PROCEDURE, PROFILE, ROLE, ROLLBACK SEGMENT, SCHEMA, SEQUENCE, SNAPSHOT, SNAPSHOT LOG, SYNONYM

- CREATE TABLE RECOVERABLE

- CREATE TRIGGER, USER, VIEW

- DELETE, DROP, INDEX, DROP PACKAGE, PROCEDURE, PROFILE, ROLE, ROLLBACK SEGMENT, SEQUENCE, SNAPSHOT, SNAPSHOT LOG, SYNONYM

- DROP TABLE, TABLESPACE, TRIGGER, VIEW, USER

- EXPLAIN PLAN, GRANT, INSERT, LOCK TABLE, NOAUDIT, RENAME, REVOKE, ROLLBACK, SAVEPOINT, SELECT, SET ROLE, SET TRANSACTION, TRUNCATE, UPDATE.

The following commands **will not be propagated**:

- sqlldr direct=false (using the UNRECOVERABLE option)

- ALTER DATABASE ADD LOGFILE, ADD LOGFILE MEMBER, CREATE DATAFILE, DISABLE, DISABLE THREAD, ENABLE THREAD, DROP LOGFILE MEMBER, DROP LOGFILE GROUP, RENAME FILE, RENAME GLOBAL_NAME

- ALTER INDEX REBUILD UNRECOVERABLE

- ALTER TABLESPACE ADD DATAFILE, RENAME DATAFILE

- CREATE DATABASE

- CREATE INDEX REBUILD UNRECOVERABLE

- CREATE TABLE UNRECOVERABLE

- CREATE TABLESPACE

The following commands **will invalidate** the hot standby database. In this case the database will have to be rebuilt:

- ALTER DATABASE BACKUP CONTROLFILE TO TRACE – only invalidates the hot standby if the database is subsequently opened with the RESETLOGS option.

- ALTER DATABASE CONVERT, CLEAR LOGFILE, NOARCHIVELOG, OPEN RESETLOGS

- ALTER DATABASE RECOVER AUTOMATIC, DATAFILE, LOGFILE, TABLESPACE, UNTIL CANCEL, UNTIL TIME, UNTIL CHANGE, USING BACKUP CONTROLFILE – if recovery can be performed without resetting the logs the standby database will not be invalidated.

- ALTER DATABASE RESET COMPATIBILITY

- ALTER SYSTEM ARCHIVE LOG STOP

- CREATE CONTROLFILE – will invalidate the hot standby database if the archive stream is interrupted.

7.1.3 How the SAP utilities support the hot standby database

Both BRARCHIVE and BRBACKUP support the hot standby database concept as follows:

- BRARCHIVE is able to copy the archived redo logs from the primary machine to the secondary machine. It will also check that the copy has worked successfully.

- BRARCHIVE will automatically execute the RECOVER STANDBY DATABASE command causing Oracle to apply the recently copied redo logs to the hot standby database data files.

- BRBACKUP can backup the standby database.

- BRBACKUP can be used to create another standby database and to rebuild the production database after a switchover.

Using BRARCHIVE in a hot standby database scenario

In a hot standby database scenario, BRARCHIVE is used to copy the archived redo logs from the production database to the hot standby database. This is possible because BRARCHIVE is able to make copies to disk.

The way this works is shown in Figure 7.2. A BRARCHIVE process runs on the primary machine and copies the archived redo logs from the production system to a mounted directory on the secondary machine (usually /oracle/<SID>/saparch). This copy will,

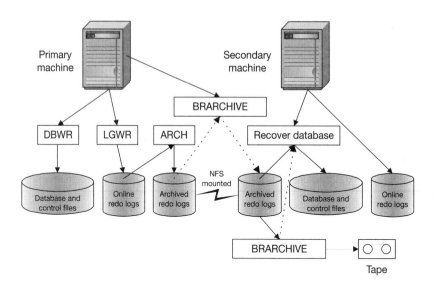

Figure 7.2   BRARCHIVE in an Oracle standby database architecture

therefore, take place over a network so it is recommended to use the -w switch on the
BRARCHIVE command line so that the file copy is verified.

A BRARCHIVE process also runs on the secondary machine and waits for archived
redo logs to be copied to the saparch directory. When this occurs BRARCHIVE will execute the recover standby database command causing Oracle to apply the contents of
the log to the hot standby database data files. On successful completion the archived redo
log will be backed up and automatically deleted if necessary. It is possible to delay the
application of the redo logs to the database by using the -m switch on the BRBACKUP
command line. This will avoid logical errors, such as the dropping of a table, from being
automatically propagated to the hot standby database.

Using BRBACKUP in a hot standby database scenario

The main advantage of using BRBACKUP in a hot standby database environment, is that
backups can be performed on the secondary machine with no impact on the primary
machine. This is because the hot standby database is a near duplicate of the production
system. Only offline backups can be taken due to the fact that the hot standby database
must not be opened.

The procedure to backup the hot standby database is as follows:

- In the init<SID>.sap file the backup_type parameter must be set to offline_standby.

- Execute BRBACKUP. The program will log on to the production database on the primary machine and retrieve information about the database structure. This information
  will be written to the backup log. The connection string BRBACKUP should use must
  be defined by the primary_db parameter in the init<SID>.sap file.

- The hot standby database is stopped.

- The standby database is restarted by issuing the `startup nomount` and `ALTER DATABASE MOUNT STANDBY DATABASE` commands.

Once BRBACKUP is started on the secondary machine, all subsequent steps are performed automatically.

Should you suffer a failure of your production R/3 system and you have to switchover to the hot standby it is possible to repair the previously productive system and make it the standby database. This can be performed using BRBACKUP with a `backup_type = offline_stop`. Similarly, a new standby database can be created by setting the parameter `backup_dev_type = disk_standby`.

Please note that in the event of a switchover, SAP recommends that you take a complete online backup of the 'new' production system, including the control file, once all redo data has been applied and the database is fully open.

7.2   The SAP Zero Downtime Project

The Zero Downtime Project is SAP's high availability project. The goal of this project is to reduce to a minimum both the planned and unplanned downtime of the R/3 system. SAP are achieving this by working with their main partners to develop software and hardware solutions for their customers. One outcome of this partnership has been that hardware partners now provide automatic switchover systems as required for the hot standby database architecture described in the previous section. These switchover solutions consist of two identical servers, sharing a common set of disks. When the primary server fails, the switchover software will automatically route users and work processes to the secondary server transparently. This switchover mostly works by dynamically assigning work processes to TCP/IP addresses using aliases. In this environment you will require an additional SAP license for the secondary server.

When considering the availability options for your R/3 system, you should consider the following:

- Do you need to insure against unplanned downtime?

- Can you recover sufficiently quickly from an R/3 system outage?

- How much planned downtime do you require for maintenance, hardware/software upgrades? Is this acceptable to the business?

- Does the R/3 system need to be available 24 hours a day, 7 days per week?

- What disaster recovery measures are already in place?

- How much additional work is required to maintain a switchover system?

For more detailed information on the SAP Zero Downtime Project visit SAPnet on the web at *http://sapnet.sap-ag.de*.

7.3 Critical SAP R/3 maintenance steps

As with any complex application (and they don't come any more complex than SAP R/3), it is essential to have a rigorous maintenance routine. For most, if not all companies, R/3 is one of the core applications that must always be available if it is to serve the business as it is intended. Downtime of any core system can be disastrous to the financial health of a company. As the DBA, a large part of this responsibility is yours!

In order to keep SAP R/3 running smoothly, you must bear the following points in mind:

- Make sure all routine maintenance tasks are done promptly. Daily backups must be done daily!

- Follow the SAP recommended backup schedule (see Chapter 5).

- A workable backup strategy is essential for minimizing unplanned downtime.

- Always practice database recoveries before making them part of your backup/recovery strategy. Many customers have lost data because the DBA was unable to perform the correct recovery procedure.

- Make sure you have enough pre-configured disks so that you can expand your database easily.

- Monitor tablespace growth and make sure none of the R/3 tablespaces reaches more than 85% full.

- Consider implementing a disaster recovery scenario in case the unthinkable happens and you lose your entire production system.

- If you already have a disaster recovery procedure in place, test it at least once a year. New versions of R/3 and/or Oracle may require changes to your backup and recovery strategy. Applying old procedures to new versions may make things worse, or may not work at all. Do not wait for a disaster to happen before you find this out.

8 Backup and recovery examples

Now that our discussion of SAP R/3 backup and recovery is complete, let's put it all together and consider some recovery scenarios that you may encounter in your day-to-day running of R/3. These examples should help you to understand all of the concepts we have discussed in this book and to show you how they are applied to a real-life disaster.

Some of these examples have been taken from real-life problems encountered by R/3 and Oracle customers. The following problems are discussed:

- *Example 1* – Loss of an Oracle SYSTEM tablespace data file.
- *Example 2* – Loss of a data file containing rollback segments.
- *Example 3* – Loss of a non-SYSTEM tablespace data file.
- *Example 4* – Loss of an online redo log that was not archived.
- *Example 5* – Loss of a partition in Oracle8.
- *Example 6* – How to recover using point-in-time recovery after a system clock change.
- *Example 7* – Recovering after using the RESETLOGS option.
- *Example 8* – Recovering from a database crash during a backup.

For each of the above examples we discuss the problem that has occurred, the Oracle error message you might see as a symptom of the problem, and how to solve it. For some examples, we will use SAPDBA to resolve the problem, for others we will use Server Manager and/or RMAN (Oracle Recovery Manager).

Please bear in mind that whilst some of these examples have been taken from real-life, the solutions provided were run on systems that will differ from yours. If you decide to use any of these solutions, make sure you understand the implications for doing so on your system. The author and publishers cannot be held responsible for any problems so arising. These examples are provided for illustrative purposes only.

8.1 Example 1 – Loss of an Oracle SYSTEM tablespace data file

The problem

A disk containing a data file belonging to the SYSTEM tablespace crashes, causing the data file to be lost. The objective is to get the database back up and running as quickly as possible.

The error message

In this case you may see either of the following error messages:

```
ORA-01157: cannot identify data file <num> - data file not found
```

```
ORA-01147: SYSTEM tablespace file <num> is offline
```

These messages will be followed by an ORA-01110 message giving the name of the data file causing the problem.

The solution

Normally a damaged or lost data file can be taken offline and the database then restarted. Unfortunately the data file lost in this example belongs to the SYSTEM tablespace and none of the data files in this tablespace may be taken offline.

The only answer is to shutdown the database, restore the lost data file from the most recent backup and perform a recovery.

To recover individual data files in SAPDBA, select option *d – Restore individual file(s)* from the *Restore/recovery* menu. A second menu is displayed, as shown in Chapter 6 Figure 6.17.

The procedure is as follows:

- Select option *A – File type*, this will display a third menu, as seen in Chapter 6 Figure 6.18.

- To restore data files select option *b – Data files* from the menu then select option *q – Return* to go back to the previous menu.

- Next select option *b – BRBACKUP run* to select the backup from which the required data file(s) are to be copied.

- Select option *c – Enter/show files*. A list of files available from the backup selected in option *b* will be displayed. Select the required file from this list, the status will be set to *Res yes* indicating that it will be restored.

- To start the restore select option *S – Start BRRESTORE*. As this option indicates, the BRRESTORE utility will be used to copy the chosen file(s) from the backup device(s). If files with the same name already exist, you will be prompted to indicate whether you want them overwritten or not. Select the *yes* option.

- During the restore, various messages will be displayed including prompts for the operator to mount the required tape(s). All activities are logged to a file called <timestamp>.dba in the /oracle/<SID>/sapreorg directory.

- On successful completion of the restore the recovery process will have to be started from the *Check (and repair) database* menu in SAPDBA.

- On successful completion of the recovery the database will be reopened.

During this process the R/3 system and database will be unavailable.

8.2   Example 2 – Loss of a data file containing rollback segments

The problem

Due to a media failure a data file belonging to the rollback segment tablespace is lost. Our objective is to recover the data file without loss of the undo data contained in the rollback segments.

The error message

Several error messages could be encountered for this problem. One that is commonly seen is:

```
ORA-00376: file <num> cannot be read at this time
```

The file number specified in this message points to the data file Oracle was trying to read, which in our example would be a data file containing rollback segments. This error is usually followed by an ORA-01110 error, which gives the name of the file that cannot be read.

The solution

Media recovery needs to be performed on the rollback segment data files. To do this, all data files belonging to the tablespace must be taken offline whilst the database is mounted. If you wish to allow R/3 users to continue using the database whilst recovering the rollback segment tablespace, you will need to open the database and create some temporary rollback segments in another tablespace. This will allow R/3 to begin running again whilst you perform the recovery.

The procedure, using Server Manager, is as follows:

- Manually edit the init<SID>.ora initialization file and comment out the ROLLBACK_SEGMENTS parameter.

- Mount the database using the command startup mount.

- Take the rollback segment tablespace data files offline using the command ALTER DATABASE DATAFILE '<data filename>' OFFLINE.

- Reopen the database using the command ALTER DATABASE OPEN.

- Create temporary rollback segments in another tablespace and bring them online using these commands:

    ```
    CREATE ROLLBACK SEGMENT <temp rollback segment name> TABLESPACE
    <tablespace name>

    ALTER ROLLBACK SEGMENT <temp rollback segment name> ONLINE
    ```

    These commands should be executed for every rollback segment you create.

- Restore the data file from a backup copy. You may use a UNIX `tar` or `cpio` command to do this. You may also need to restore the archived redo logs as well.

- Recover the tablespace using the command `RECOVER TABLESPACE <tablespace name>`.

- Bring the tablespace back online using the command `ALTER TABLESPACE <table-space name> ONLINE`.

- Bring the recovered rollback segments back online by executing `ALTER ROLLBACK SEGMENT <rollback segment name> ONLINE` for each rollback segment.

- Manually edit the Oracle initialization file and uncomment the `ROLLBACK_SEGMENTS` parameter.

- At a convenient time take the temporary rollback segments offline and drop them using these commands for each temporary rollback segment:

    ```
    ALTER ROLLBACK SEGMENT <temp rollback segment name> OFFLINE
    ```

    ```
    DROP ROLLBACK SEGMENT <temp rollback segment name>
    ```

The above procedure can be implemented with RMAN, as shown in Figure 8.1.

```
RMAN> run {
2> allocate channel dev1 type 'tape';
3> restore datafile <data filename>;
4> recover tablespace <rollback segment tablespace name>;
5> sql 'alter tablespace <rollback segment tablespace name>
6> online';
7> }
```

Figure 8.1   Recovering rollback segments using RMAN

We could also have used the `RECOVER DATAFILE` command to recover the damaged data file individually.

8.3   Example 3 – Loss of a non-SYSTEM tablespace data file

The problem

A data file belonging to one of the SAP R/3 data tablespaces is lost due to a disk crash. The objective is to recover the data file as quickly as possible.

The error message

The same message would be seen as described for example 2 above. The ORA-00376 followed by ORA-01110 giving the name of the data file that could not be accessed.

The solution

The fact that an R/3 database runs in ARCHIVELOG mode means that you have several solutions to this problem. If you were to perform the restore and recovery manually you could use one of the following commands:

- RECOVER DATABASE – which would require an offline recovery to be performed because the database must be mounted but not open. Not recommended just to recover a single data file!

- RECOVER TABLESPACE – this is performed with the database open but the tablespace offline. This procedure was described in example 2.

- RECOVER DATAFILE – this will recover only the damaged data file whilst the database is open. It may be possible in an Oracle8 partitioned tablespace for the unaffected partitions to still be used by R/3 whilst recovery of the lost data file is taking place. This is the preferred solution for our example.

The solution detailed here is very similar to the solution given for example 1, with the exception that the database can remain open throughout the restore/recovery process.
The procedure is as follows:

- Take the damaged data file offline using the command ALTER DATABASE DATAFILE <data filename> OFFLINE.

- In SAPDBA, select option *d – Restore individual file(s)* from the *Restore/recovery* menu. A second menu is displayed, as shown in Chapter 6 Figure 6.17.

- Select option *a – File type*, this will display a third menu, as seen in Chapter 6 Figure 6.18.

- To restore data files select option *b – Data files* from the menu then select option *q – Return* to go back to the previous menu.

- Next select option *b – BRBACKUP run* to select the backup from which the required data file(s) are to be copied.

- Select option *c – Enter/show files*. A list of files available from the backup selected in option *b* will be displayed. Select the required file from this list, the status will be set to *Res yes* indicating that it will be restored.

- To start the restore select option *S – Start BRRESTORE*. As this option indicates, the BRRESTORE utility will be used to copy the chosen file(s) from the backup device(s). If files with the same name already exist, you will be prompted to indicate whether you want them overwritten or not. Select the *yes* option.

- During the restore, various messages will be displayed including prompts for the operator to mount the required tape(s). All activities are logged to a file called `<timestamp>.dba` in the `/oracle/<SID>/sapreorg` directory.

- On successful completion of the restore the recovery process will have to be started from the *Check (and repair) database* menu in SAPDBA.

8.4   Example 4 – Loss of an online redo log that was not archived

The problem

A power outage causes the Oracle database to crash. When the database is restarted an error indicates that an online redo log cannot be read. All data files and the current control file are undamaged. The lost online redo log has not yet been archived. The objective is to restore to as close to the time of the loss as possible.

The error message

The error messages you will most likely see when this type of failure occurs are:

`ORA-00313: open failed for members of log group <num> of thread <num>`

`ORA-00312: online log <num> thread <num>: <online log filename>`

The first message tells you that Oracle cannot open an online redo log file and the second message gives you the name and location of that file.

The solution

Whilst the data files are intact they cannot be used because crash recovery cannot be performed due to the loss of the online redo log. Instead, media recovery needs to be performed.

Under any normal R/3 operation this situation should never occur because in an R/3 installation Oracle maintains mirrored copies of each online redo log. Having said this, the author has experience of visiting various SAP sites to find that the online redo logs, and their mirrored copies, have been installed on disks using the same disk controller. In this case, should a controller fail, the mirrored copies of the online redo logs are lost as well! To avoid this, make sure your online mirrored redo logs are sitting on disks accessed by different disk controllers.

To recover from this situation, all data files and archived redo logs from the last consistent online or offline backup must be restored and a roll forward applied up to the last available redo log prior to the online redo log file loss. This will be an *incomplete recovery* and may result in loss of data. The only option is to perform a database level recovery.

The procedure, using Server Manager, is as follows:

- Make sure the R/3 system is stopped. Shut Oracle down by executing the command `shutdown abort`.

- Restore all data files and archived redo log files (if necessary) using either the UNIX `tar` or `cpio` commands.

- Mount the database using the command `startup mount`.

- Perform database recovery using the command `RECOVER DATABASE UNTIL CANCEL`.

- Keep pressing the "Enter" key until you either receive the message `ORA-00278: Logfile <name> no longer needed for this recovery`, or until you have applied the last log sequence number prior to the crash. At this point enter the keyword `CANCEL` which will stop the recovery process.

- Reopen the database using the command `ALTER DATABASE OPEN RESETLOGS`. Because we have to use the `RESETLOGS` parameter we must now perform a complete online or offline backup of the database, including the current control file, as recommended by SAP. Any previous backups are no longer valid.

Please note, instead of using the `UNTIL CANCEL` option to recover the database, we could have used `UNTIL TIME`, to restore to a specific date and time, or `UNTIL CHANGE`, to restore up to a specific SCN.

We could also have performed this recovery using the database recovery option in SAPDBA. Please refer to the section in Chapter 6 headed **Recovering the database** (p. 131), for a detailed discussion.

8.5 Example 5 – Loss of a partition in Oracle8

The problem

A table, consisting of four partitions in an Oracle8 database, loses one of its partitions due to a disk failure. Each partition is located in a different tablespace and each tablespace is located on a different disk. The objective is to recover the lost partition whilst maintaining maximum availability of the remaining partitions.

The error message

Whilst R/3 is selecting data from the table the following errors will appear:

```
ORA-00376: file <num> cannot be read at this time

ORA-01110: data file <num>: <name>
```

The solution

The table is partitioned with each partition sitting in a different tablespace. In turn each of these tablespaces resides on a different disk. In this case we can simply recover the lost partition whilst the rest of the table can still be accessed by R/3. There is no need to stop R/3 or the database.

To recover the partition we simply perform a tablespace recovery. The procedure is:

- Restore the tablespace (partition) data file(s).

- Recover the tablespace using the RECOVER TABLESPACE command.

- Bring the tablespace (partition) back online using the command ALTER TABLESPACE <tablespace name> ONLINE.

This procedure can easily be implemented using either SAPDBA or RMAN. Figure 8.2 shows how it is implemented using RMAN.

```
RMAN> run {
2> allocate channel dev1 type 'tape';
3> restore datafile <data filename>;
4> recover tablespace <tablespace name>;
5> sql 'alter tablespace <tablespace name> online';
6> }
```

Figure 8.2   Recovering an Oracle8 partition using RMAN

8.6   Example 6 – How to recover using point-in-time recovery after a system clock change

The problem

A table becomes corrupted due to a disk problem. A point-in–time recovery is needed to recover the table to a point just before the corruption. The table has to be restored from a backup but the problem is that between the time of the backup and the corruption of the table, the system clock was put back one hour.

When trying to perform point-in-time recovery through a system clock change, problems can occur. This concept can be difficult to follow so to make it a little clearer it will help if you refer to Figure 8.3 below.

This figure shows several transactions and the times they occurred. Point A indicates where the backup was taken, point B shows where the system clock was changed, and point C is where the table corruption occurred.

The error message

The most likely error message encountered when a table is corrupted will be:

ORA-1578 Data block corrupted in file #<num> block #<num>

This is usually accompanied by an ORA-600 internal error written to the Oracle alert log.

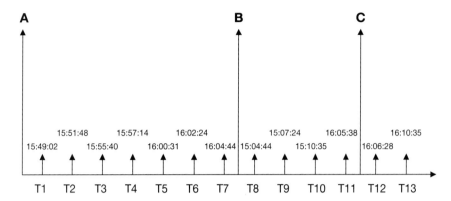

Figure 8.3   Database transaction timeline

The solution

To recover the table we would need to reapply the changes from the redo logs up to the point of failure, but before the corruption. Normally to do this you would use the RECOVER DATABASE UNTIL TIME command specifying the time at which recovery is to stop.

The problem here is that, depending on the time you specify, not all of the redo will be reapplied as expected. For example, using the timings seen in Figure 8.3 above, if we execute the following command:

```
RECOVER DATABASE UNTIL '1999-01-08:16:05:00'
```

Oracle will recover transactions T1 through T10 (T11 is marked with a time of 16:05:38). The reason for this is that Oracle determines which redo changes to apply by the SCN **and timestamp** of each redo record, reading them sequentially from the redo log. Therefore, if you were to specify a time of 16:04:00 in the RECOVER DATABASE command, Oracle would only apply transactions T1 through T6 (T7 is marked 16:04:44). All transactions between T7 and the point of failure would potentially be lost even though the transactions after the system time change have a timestamp prior to 16:05.

It is worth noting that if you performed a complete recovery all transactions would be applied. However, depending on how the problem occurred, the corruption could be reapplied as well!

To still perform point-in-time recovery, and avoid losing the transactions between T7 and the point of failure, Oracle recommends you perform cancel-based (using UNTIL CANCEL) or change-based (using UNTIL CHANGE) recovery to the point in time where the clock is set back, then continue with the time-based recovery to the exact time.

To prevent having to face this problem, it is recommended by Oracle that you always perform a full backup of your database after a system time change.

8.7   Example 7 – Recovering after using the RESETLOGS option

The problem

A crash occurs after having opened the database using the RESETLOGS option. The only backup available is a full database backup taken prior to the redo logs being reset. The objective is to recover the database without loss of data.

The error message

We have not specified the type of crash that has occurred in this example. It could be the loss of an individual table, a data file, a complete tablespace, or the entire database. The actual type of crash is irrelevant for our purposes so therefore we are not discussing a particular error message here. It could be one of many.

The solution

Both SAP and Oracle strongly recommend that either a full offline or online backup be taken **immediately** after having opened the database with the RESETLOGS option. The reason for this will become clear in our following discussion. If it is not possible to perform the backup and you then get a database failure, this solution provides two workarounds, supported by Oracle, which you can use to recover from the failure.

This solution is not an alternative for failing to backup and should only be used in an absolute emergency.

Figure 8.4 shows the sequence of events that have occurred in our example. At point A a full backup was taken, at point B the database was reopened with the RESETLOGS option, at point C the database failed. No further backups were taken between point A and point C.

The problem we have is that if we restore the database data files from the backup taken at point A and recover using the current control file, Oracle will complain that some of the data files are from a point before B and will not be able to recover them. You may think the alternative is to just restore the backup control file and recover. The problem you will then encounter is that Oracle will complain that the first data file is from a point after B,

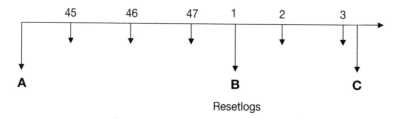

Figure 8.4   Redo log generation sequence

because the SCN number in the data file header will be higher than the SCN in the backup control file. The third option you may then try is to restore both the data files and the control file from the backup and recover. This time the problem will be that you cannot recover beyond point B because Oracle will not recognize any of the redo logs beyond this point. We will have lost, therefore, all the data entered between point B and C.

It would seem that without taking a backup between point B and C, we have to resign ourselves to the fact that we have lost data. This is not necessarily the case. A new feature implemented in Oracle 7.3.3 and higher allows the DBA to restore a database through a RESETLOGS if no consistent backup is available after the RESETLOGS. You can only use this feature if the following conditions are true:

- you are recovering an Oracle 7.3.3 and higher database;

- you have a consistent hot or cold database backup taken prior to RESETLOGS;

- you have a control file that was created after the RESETLOGS;

- all archived and online redo logs are intact.

If you meet the above conditions then you can perform one of two possible procedures to recover. The first procedure, recommended by Oracle, is as follows:

1. Before reopening the database at point B, take a cold backup of all the data files and control file.

2. Mount the database using the command startup mount.

3. Open the database using the command ALTER DATABASE OPEN RESETLOGS.

Should you then experience a failure (point C in our example) after having opened the database, you can restore **the data files** from the backup taken just before the RESETLOGS and recover using the **current control file** after point B as usual.

The second procedure provides a solution if you only have the backup available from point A in our example. It is a little more involved and is performed using the **control file available after point B**. The procedure is as follows:

1. Find out the value of the SCN immediately prior to the database being opened with RESETLOGS. The value will be reported in the Oracle alert log just before a message that says RESETLOGS after complete recovery UNTIL CHANGE <SCN number> or RESETLOGS after incomplete recovery UNTIL CHANGE <SCN number>. Compare this SCN number with the value returned from the following query:

    ```
    SELECT RESETLOGS_CHANGE# - 1 FROM V$DATABASE;
    ```

    These values should be identical. This is the SCN value you use for recovery.

2. Shut down the database using the command SHUTDOWN.

3. Copy the current control file to a safe location. This must be the control file created **after** RESETLOGS. Also backup all archived redo logs for safety.

4. Restore the whole database and control file from the backup before the RESETLOGS (point A in our example).

5. Recover the database using the command RECOVER DATABASE USING BACKUP CON-TROLFILE UNTIL CHANGE <SCN number>. Replace <SCN number> with the SCN value you obtained in step 1.

6. After successful recovery, shut down the database.

7. Copy the control file you saved in step 3 to **all** locations as specified in the CONTROL_FILES parameter in the Oracle initialization file. In other words, you are overwriting the backup control file and all mirror copies.

8. Mount the database using the command startup mount.

9. Use the RECOVER DATABASE command, with the appropriate option for your needs, and recover normally. Oracle will now ask for redo log number 1 and will apply all redo changes made since the RESETLOGS (point B in our example). It may be possible that you have some redo log sequence numbers from before the RESETLOGS that are the same as those generated after the RESETLOGS. Make sure you do not overwrite them when restoring from your backup.

For extra safety, Oracle recommends the following best practices when using the RESET-LOGS option:

- always backup the database immediately after a RESETLOGS. The solution described above is not a real substitute for a backup;

- always backup the control file after a RESETLOGS, especially if you are not able to do a full database backup immediately;

- backup the Oracle alert log after performing a RESETLOGS;

- protect any backups taken before a RESETLOGS until the next full backup is taken after the RESETLOGS;

- backup all archived and online redo logs used for recovery **before** opening the database with RESETLOGS.

8.8   Example 8 – Recovering from a database crash during a backup

The problem

During a hot backup of a tablespace, the machine on which the R/3 database is running goes down, taking the database with it. When the machine is rebooted, restarting Oracle gives an error indicating that media recovery is required. On large R/3 systems with several hundred redo logs, recovery can take a long time. The objective is to recover from the crash as quickly as possible.

The error message

The error messages that will be seen in this situation are:

```
ORA-01113: file <num> needs media recovery
```

```
ORA-01110: data file <num>: <name>
```

The first message indicates the number of the file that requires recovery and the second one tells you the name and location of the file.

The solution

This solution will only work on Oracle version 7.2 databases and above. Prior to this release, recovery from this situation was unnecessarily complicated and took a long time. The new functionality Oracle introduced gives the DBA the ability to execute the ALTER DATABASE DATAFILE '<data filename>' END BACKUP whilst the database is mounted but not open. The significance of this is that after this command is executed and the database reopened no recovery is required, therefore the database can be made available immediately.

The solution is as follows:

- Mount the database using the command startup mount.

- End the backup on the appropriate file using the command ALTER DATABASE DATAFILE '<data filename>' END BACKUP.

- Open the database with the command ALTER DATABASE OPEN.

The reason why Oracle does not have to perform recovery on the data file is because when a tablespace is placed in hot backup mode only some data structures in the file headers are updated, others are frozen. This was discussed in Chapter 6 in the sections discussing Oracle7 and Oracle8 data file headers. The contents of the data file, however, are current because Oracle does not block updates from being written into the data file during a hot backup. When a checkpoint is performed, the *Checkpointed at SCN* value is not updated in the data file header. When the tablespace is taken out of backup mode, all Oracle has to do is to update the data file headers with the correct SCN value. Executing the ALTER DATABASE DATAFILE '<data filename>' END BACKUP command does this.

This feature saves a great deal of time and effort should you experience a database crash during a hot backup.

9 Future trends and directions

This final chapter discusses those changes, future trends and directions that the author perceives are likely to affect the backup and recovery strategy of most, if not all, companies who use SAP R/3 in the future.

9.1 Shrinking batch windows, growing databases

Perhaps one of the biggest problems today's DBA faces is the rapidly reducing batch window. SAP R/3 databases are growing out of all proportion, more and more data is being kept online, and more companies are making their R/3 systems available 24 hours a day, 7 days a week.

As an R/3 database grows, so does the length of time it takes to back it up. Traditionally, DBAs have preferred to backup their databases whilst R/3 is shutdown, and the database is unavailable to end-users. This was due to the fact that in earlier releases of Oracle, online backups were not always as reliable as they should have been. Time was always made available during the evening batch processing to allow the DBA to perform routine offline backups and maintenance as required. Today, this is not the case. In fact with the advent of Oracle8, the idea of always performing a reliable online backup became a reality. This, coupled with the fact that more and more work is being performed on behalf of the business during what was, previously, the time allotted for database maintenance, has forced more DBAs to take advantage of technologies that allow online backups to be carried out easily, quickly and reliably.

In the future we shall see R/3 databases not in the gigabytes, in terms of their size, but in the terabytes, and in the not too distant future, petabytes. This in itself will pose several problems:

- The backup/recovery tools supplied with the database will not be enhanced quickly enough to support the increased amount of data they will be required to backup. Therefore backups will be too slow, and take too long.

- No downtime of a core R/3 system will be acceptable to a business. The cost of any downtime could be the difference between a healthy profit and bankruptcy. Consider, for example, how long an airline could be without its ticketing system.

- Faster tape throughput will be required to handle the huge volumes of data being backed up.

- Third-party vendors will be stretched to keep their new releases in line with the performance, reliability and functionality needs of their customers, and therefore such tools will be behind the needs of the R/3 market.

These problems, in turn, will lead to the following situations occurring:

- All backups and recoveries will have to be performed online whilst both the database and R/3 are fully functional.

- There will be an increase in the use of hardware- and software-based switchover systems supporting hot standby and failover database technologies.

- More hardware will be purchased to handle the ever-increasing data volume requirements and backups will be performed from machine to machine with tape backups being performed offline.

- DBAs will be selective about the database objects they backup. It will become harder to perform full database, or even tablespace, backups within an acceptable time period.

- Emphasis will be on speed and reliability of backups.

- Timely recoveries will become harder to implement given the potential volume of data that will need to be restored.

- There will be an increasing use of parallel backup and parallel recovery technology to make backup/recovery even faster. This will add another level of complexity to the management of the R/3 database for the DBA.

- More R/3 systems will move from a centralized to a distributed architecture, organized by function, to try and contain the amount of data held in any one location. This will make backups and recoveries more manageable, but will increase the complexity of managing R/3.

- Faster network topologies will be required to support the R/3 distributed architecture.

To solve these issues, companies will need to consider how they can implement online backups and fast recoveries whilst running a 24x7 system. This will only be achieved by implementing hot standby systems, introducing advanced failover hardware and software, making more use of parallel server technology, and implementing technology that allows DBAs to handle distributed backups and recoveries from one central location, reliably.

One added complication I haven't mentioned is the internet and intranet. At the time of writing, Oracle are about to release Oracle 8i, the next generation database for the web. SAP have not yet announced how they will support this technology, but one thing is sure, any backup and recovery strategy you have in place today will need to be re-written once this new database is in general use.

Without doubt, a SAP R/3 DBA has some very interesting times ahead. Hopefully this book has already helped to prepare for those times, and will continue to do so for a very long time to come.

Bibliography

Advanced Information Systems, Inc., et al. *Oracle Unleashed (second edition)*. Sams Publishing, 1997.

Chlond, G., Steinmaier, C. *Oracle Standby Database Scenario*. SAP AG, 1998.

Chlond, G., Steinmaier, C. *Split Mirror Disk Backup*. SAP AG, 1998.

Chlond, G., Steinmaier, C., Volkmann, K. *Oracle Recovery Manager Integration into SAPDBA*. SAP AG, 1998.

Chlond, G., Steinmaier, C. *Disaster Recovery for SAP R/3 on Oracle*. SAP AG, 1998.

Greene, J. *Oracle8 Server Unleashed*. Sams Publishing, 1998.

Hernandez, J.A. *The SAP R/3 Handbook*. McGraw-Hill, 1997.

Loney, K. *Oracle DBA Handbook*. Oracle Press, Osborne/McGraw-Hill, 1994.

Oracle Corporation. *Oracle7 Server Administration*. Oracle Corporation, 1997.

Oracle Corporation. *Oracle7 Parallel Server Administrators' Guide*. Oracle Corporation, 1997.

Oracle Corporation. *Oracle7 Messages and Codes Manual*. Oracle Corporation, 1997.

Oracle Corporation. *Oracle8 Server Administration*. Oracle Corporation, 1998.

Oracle Corporation. *Oracle8 Parallel Server Concepts and Administration*. Oracle Corporation, 1998.

Oracle Corporation. *Oracle8 Server Utilities*. Oracle Corporation, 1998.

Oracle Corporation. *Oracle8 Messages and Codes Manual*. Oracle Corporation, 1998.

SAP AG. *SAP Tools to Backup the Oracle Database*. SAP AG, 1998.

SAP AG. *Introducing R/3 on Oracle Parallel Server*. SAP AG, 1997.

SAP AG. *BC-BRI Backint Interface for Oracle Databases*. SAP AG, 1997.

SAP AG. *R/3 Installation on UNIX, Oracle Parallel Server*. SAP AG, 1997.

SAP AG. *R/3 Backup Strategy*. SAP AG, 1998.

Velpuri, R., Adkoli, A. *Oracle8 Backup and Recovery Handbook*. Oracle Press, Osborne/McGraw-Hill, 1998.

Will, L., et al. *SAP R/3 Administration*. Addison Wesley Longman, 1998.

Index